MW00579032

Days Are Coming
A Journey through the Jewish Year

מגיד

MAGGID

Sivan Rahav-Meir

DAYS ARE COMING

**A Journey through
the Jewish Year**

TRANSLATED BY

Yehoshua Siskin

Maggid Books

Days Are Coming
A Journey through the Jewish Year

First Edition, 2022

Maggid Books
An imprint of Koren Publishers Jerusalem Ltd.

POB 8531, New Milford, CT 06776-8531, USA
& POB 4044, Jerusalem 9104001, Israel
www.maggidbooks.com

The publication of this book was made possible
through the generous support of *The Jewish Book Trust*.

ISBN 978-1-59264-602-9, *hardcover*

Printed and bound in the United States

In honor of
Andrew Lewis

חנוך ראובן

for his Diamond Jubilee Birthday!

וַיִּתְהַלֵּךְ חֲנוֹךְ אֶת־הָאֱלֹהִים...
"Hanoch walked faithfully with God…"

May our Hanoch always walk with Hashem and live a long life.

~

For an aliyah of the neshamot of

אברהם בן בן־ציון הלוי ז״ל
שושנה בת פאול ז״ל
רחמה בת חנוך ראובן ז״ל
דניאל דוד בן נפתלי הרץ ז״ל

~

And for a merit that all Jewish singles meet their *zivugim*.

"האירה את העולם בתורה ובמעשים טובים"

In loving memory of
Katie Fishel

Whose sense of humor kept those around her smiling,
whose passion for shidduchim kept those around her hoping,
and whose generosity of heart let everyone in her presence know
she was there for them.

In her short life Katie brought joy to so many through her thoughtfulness.
Her love and kindness for family and friends knew no bounds.
She will always be cherished.

לעילוי נשמת
מאירה חיה נחמה ברכה ע"ה
בת דוד מרדכי וזעלדה שיינדל שיחיו
1/26/1998 – 11/23/2018
כ"ט טבת תשנ"ח - ט"ו כסלו תשע"ט
יהי זכרה ברוך

Contents

Introduction   xiii

ELUL
First of Elul   1
September 1: Back to School   6
Third of Elul: Anniversary of the Death of Rav Kook   9
Eighteenth of Elul   11

TISHREI
Rosh HaShana   15
Third of Tishrei: Fast of Gedalia   19
Ten Days of Teshuva   20
Yom Kippur   25
Yom Kippur Prayers   30
Sukkot   34
Ḥol HaMoed (Intermediate Days of Sukkot)   39
Simḥat Torah   42
Aḥarei HaḤagim (After the Holidays)   44

ḤESHVAN
Third of Ḥeshvan: Anniversary of the
Death of Rabbi Ovadia Yosef   47

Seventh of Ḥeshvan 49

Eleventh of Ḥeshvan: Anniversary of the
Death of Our Matriarch Rachel 52

Twenty-Ninth of Ḥeshvan: Sigd 53

KISLEV

Nineteenth of Kislev 57

Hanukka 60

Zot Ḥanukka (This Is Hanukka) 71

TEVET

Tenth of Tevet 73

Twentieth of Tevet: Anniversary of Maimonides's Death 77

SHEVAT

Tu BiShvat (Fifteenth of Shevat) 79

First Semester Report Cards 83

Shabbat Shira (Sabbath of Song) 85

ADAR

First of Adar 89

Seventh of Adar: Anniversary of the Death of Moses 92

Shabbat Zakhor (Sabbath of Remembrance) 94

Taanit Esther (Fast of Esther) 95

Purim 97

NISAN

Blessing the Fruit Trees 105

Preparations for Passover 106

Shabbat HaGadol (The Great Sabbath) 109

The Festival of Passover 110

The Passover Haggada 115

Shevi'i shel Pesaḥ (Seventh Day of Passover) 127

Mimouna   129

Returning to Routine   131

Sefirat HaOmer (Counting the Omer)   132

Yom HaShoah – Holocaust Martyrs' and Heroes' Remembrance Day   135

IYAR

*Yom HaZikaron – Memorial Day for Israel's Fallen
Soldiers and Victims of Terrorism*   145

Yom HaAtzma'ut – Independence Day   150

Pesaḥ Sheni (Second Passover)   157

Lag BaOmer   158

Twenty-Eighth of Iyar: Yom Yerushalayim (Jerusalem Day)   163

SIVAN

Entering the Month of Sivan   169

Shavuot   170

TAMUZ

Third of Tamuz   181

Seventeenth of Tamuz   185

Between the Straits   187

AV

The Nine Days   191

Shabbat Ḥazon (Sabbath of Vision)   194

Tisha B'Av   195

Shabbat Naḥamu (Sabbath of Consolation)   199

Tu B'Av (Fifteenth of Av)   200

DAYS OF CORONA

Pandemic   209

2020 Does Not Deserve an X   239

Introduction

THE CYCLE OF the Jewish year is a journey, taking us through a process of growth. Each holiday highlights something special, and adds depth to different aspects of our characters. In order to truly appreciate the gifts these holidays bring, we need to know as much as possible about them. We need to prepare for them, study and learn about them. The book before you is a guide to the holidays that we encounter on our journey through the year: How are we liberated on Passover? How do we experience the true joy of Sukkot? What can we learn from Hanukka, Purim, Tu BiShvat, and the various fasts? Why do we even celebrate all the holidays and festivals, and how are they relevant to our lives in the modern world?

I have written this guide at a time of particular anxiety, both worldwide and national. In the midst of a pandemic, between one round of elections and another, it seems to me that our daily routine has been hijacked – that the cycle of the Jewish-Israeli year has been erased and forgotten among the headlines, conflicts, and stormy debates. I remember hosting a broadcast in the news studio when one of the commentators said, "The elections will be held between Purim and Passover so that the government will be formed by Shavuot." It is of course important to form a government, but the holidays are not only dates on the calendar. They are our common denominator – the past, the present, and the future.

The response to the short articles I have published on social networks about the holidays has shown me that I am not alone in feeling this way. There is a great thirst for texts that connect us to the holidays. And so this book was born. I have included a selection of my posts and columns, with added insights and articles.

The ideas are not mine. Most of them come from sages and commentators of past generations, but also from authors and thinkers of our own time. Last but not least, I have also included thoughts and observations sent to me by readers from throughout the Jewish world.

Following the journey from Tishrei to Elul, there is an additional chapter: "Days of Corona." It is a collection of thoughts and words of counsel expressed during the pandemic. I include it with the hope that we will soon be able to read it looking back, solely in the past tense, simply as a matter of historical interest.

∞

There were many partners in this project whom I want to acknowledge. First and foremost, thank you to my husband Yedidya, the engine behind it all, including this book. Thank you to our children, Aharon (for his wise comments), Tamar, Netanel, Hillel, and Yehudit.

Thank you to my dear father and mother, Aryeh and Ronit, and to Savta Rachel, who are the reason I'm here today. Thank you to my father- and mother-in-law, Rabbi Eliav and Ziva Meir, and to my brothers- and sisters-in-law for so many festivals and holidays together.

Thank you to Benayahu Yom Tov, who is much more than an agent.

Thank you to the dedicated volunteers who translate and spread the "Daily Portion" that I write into seventeen languages throughout the world. (To subscribe: www.sivanrahavmeir.com/the-daily-whatsapp/)

Thank you to my translator, Yehoshua Siskin, who translates the "Daily Portion" on a daily basis. It is a privilege that he has now translated an entire book of mine.

Thank you to Rav Moshe Weiss, for your insightful editing and inspiration.

Thank you to Shira Jacobowitz for your daily partnership in the "Daily Portion" in English.

Thank you to the Lewis family, and to the family of Katie Fishel *a"h*, who supported the publication of this English edition of the book.

A tremendous thank you to the staff of Koren Publishers. It was a pleasure working with you again: Yehoshua Miller, Matthew Miller, and Rabbi Reuven Ziegler. My thanks to Aryeh Grossman, Tani Bayer, and Tomi Mager, and editors Ita Olesker, Kate Gerstler, and Tali Simon.

Thanks to you, the readers, viewers, and responders, for the continuous feedback, both the compliments and the criticism, which helps me to constantly improve. And thank you to everyone who sends me contributions, from Israel and from around the world.

Finally, thank you to God, who sanctifies the Jewish people and the holidays.

Sivan Rahav-Meir
Jerusalem

Elul

A new beginning

The path we are taking begins here. It is the first of Elul, exactly one month before Rosh HaShana, and the summer is over. Yet this date does not signify the end of a year or season, but rather a new beginning. The month of Elul has always represented preparation and self-improvement, refining ourselves as we welcome the prospect of a good new year. Above all, Elul challenges us with a profound question: Are we capable of change? Do we truly believe that we, or indeed our reality, can be different and better? Or do we believe that everything is predetermined, that we are bound by the laws of nature and therefore powerless to change ourselves or our destiny? Do we believe in *teshuva*? *Teshuva*, after all, is not only about the level of observance of Judaism. Every act of self-improvement – however small – and every correct choice, is an act of *teshuva* as well.

In a wonderful text, often quoted during Elul, Maimonides explains the concept of free choice while highlighting the meaning of *teshuva* as it pertains to the freedom of every human being. "Free will is granted to every person. If one desires to turn to the path of good and be righteous, the choice is his. Should he desire to

1

turn to the path of evil and be wicked, the choice is his.... A person should not heed the view held by fools … and the unenlightened... that at the time of a person's creation, the Holy One, blessed be He, decrees whether he will be righteous or wicked. This is untrue.... The Creator does not decree that a person will be either good or evil.... This principle is a fundamental concept and a foundational pillar of the entire Torah and the mitzvot" (*Mishneh Torah, Hilkhot Teshuva*, chapter 5).

A campaign is needed to remind us that we are indeed autonomous beings and have free choice. We need to take the current trend that we see and reset it in the opposite direction. The algorithms of today's social networks attempt to penetrate our minds with addictive messages. Advertisements claim that "it's natural for you to have no self-control," as if we are weak and easily pulled along, and promotions for reality shows broadcast the message that we simply "must watch." Of course, sometimes it is easiest to feign misery and make excuses for our actions: "It's not my fault. Because of my parents/my teachers/my mother-in-law…I had no choice...."

The powerful gift described by Maimonides, the freedom to make choices and to change, is of course always open to us, but it is especially accessible during Elul, the prime time for this process of introspection and self-improvement. The road we are about to take starts here. Seize this extraordinary opportunity for self-development and begin your journey right now! Have a good month. Have a good year. *Shana tova.*

The first night of *Seliḥot* (prayers for divine forgiveness)

Throughout the world, Sephardic Jews begin to say *Seliḥot* at the beginning of Elul, special prayers that will continue until Yom Kippur. Rabbi Chaim Sabato described the magical *Seliḥot* he heard as a child while living in an absorption camp for new immigrants in Israel:

"Grandfather sweetly sings the *Seliḥot* prayers. There is pain in the *Seliḥot* tunes: pain of the *Shekhina* (Divine Presence), pain of the *galut* (exile), and pain that comes from sin, but there is no despair. The melodies descend to the depths of the heart and ascend to the heights of *teshuva* until they glitter with sparks of hope. And everyone cries. Some cry over the body and its ills, some cry over the soul that is tormented by sin, and some, upon hearing others cry, cry together with them.

"From the women's section, the sounds of sobbing are heard. One woman stands in a corner and sighs. Another stands in the opposite corner and weeps. Old women are sighing over their sins, pleading for an end that is favorable. Mothers are crying over their unmarried daughters.

"And then all are suddenly stirred as they read together, as if with a single heart: 'Benevolent God, compassionate and gracious One.' And then, after the *Seliḥot*, words of reconciliation are sung melodiously for the pardon that has been promised: 'For on this day you will be forgiven and cleansed from all your sins.' Whose heart would not melt on such a day?"

The world is changing. In recent years, there has been a tremendous influx of people at *Seliḥot* prayers. Participation in *Seliḥot* tours – visiting synagogues to hear different liturgical and melodic versions of *Seliḥot* – has also grown. These developments are perhaps signs of a deep yearning to reconnect with this beautiful and meaningful tradition.

When Rabbi Lau heard the shofar

Rabbi Yisrael Meir Lau once described the emotional moment he first heard the shofar blown during *Seliḥot*:

"We immigrated to Israel at the beginning of the month of Av 5705 (1945), shortly after the end of World War II. We were a group of children and youths who were orphans of the Holocaust. At the age of eight I did not know how to read or write and did

3

not understand a single word of Hebrew. Needless to say, I did not know anything about Rosh HaShana or the shofar. After a short stay in Atlit and some time spent in a children's institution in Kfar Saba, I arrived at the home of my uncle, Rabbi Mordechai Fogelman, of blessed memory, who was the rabbi of Kiryat Motzkin, near Haifa. I lived there until I reached bar mitzva age. The main synagogue was located in the center of the town. It was an impressive size with a high dome and was filled to capacity on Shabbat but sparsely attended during the week.

"I will never forget the morning when, at age eight, I accompanied my uncle to the synagogue for the Rosh Ḥodesh Elul service, which includes Hallel, the reading of the Torah, and the Musaf prayer. All I could do was stare at the pages of the prayer book since I still did not know how to read. Suddenly I jumped, gripped with panic, at the sound of an unfamiliar siren that reverberated throughout the giant synagogue and echoes in my ears to this day. In Polish, I asked my uncle to explain the meaning of this jarring siren, and thus I received my first lesson on the meaning of the shofar in Jewish law and tradition: that from the first of the month of Elul, we blow the shofar each morning in order to awaken the hearts of the people to do *teshuva*, and that the shofar does not only make the heart tremble, reminding us of the binding of Isaac and our standing at Mount Sinai, but also that its letters spell '*shipur*' (improvement), as in 'improve your deeds.' I heard all of this for the first time in my life that morning."

This story shows us that it is possible to bridge the gaps we feel may be hindering us and to make great progress in our lives. A child who, at the age of eight, did not know what a shofar was and did not understand a word of Hebrew eventually became the Chief Rabbi of Israel and one of the most prominent Jewish speakers in the world.

To go above and within

Throughout the year, much of our energy is directed externally, toward the world at large. We are preoccupied with politics, the media, social networks – everything outside of ourselves. Elul, however, calls upon us to channel our efforts in two other directions: to look above and to look within.

Above – through prayer, hope, and heartfelt request. We direct our speech not only toward people here in this world, but toward the Master of the universe.

Within – toward self-improvement. We assess ourselves to determine what attributes and behaviors we can work on. How do we spend our days? Do we invest time and effort in refining our character and nurturing our soul? Are we happy with our children's education, with how much we invest in our family life? How can we bring about real change in our daily lives? Is it possible to bring our center of gravity into our souls and turn our thoughts toward the purpose of life? It is not by chance that the main text of Yom Kippur is "We are guilty; we have betrayed." We are not concerned with what others did wrong, but with what we have done wrong.

A month for checking our accounts

The daily calendar of the Chabad movement presents a concise, thought-provoking article a day, intended to awaken us spiritually. The following thought is given for the month of Elul:

"The month of Elul is a month for checking our accounts. In order for a business to thrive and make a significant profit, its owner must check the accounts from time to time, especially to see where there have been losses due to work improperly done. The situation is similar when it comes to our spiritual work. Throughout the year, all of Israel is preoccupied with Torah, mitzvot, and building good character traits. Then the month of Elul arrives and all Jews, according to their spiritual level, must search their souls and make a true account of everything that has transpired during the year, and to understand their virtues and strengthen them, and to recognize their shortcomings so they can work to correct them. With thorough preparation in this way, one may attain a good and sweet year both physically and spiritually."

What is this soul-searching that must be done? It is not just a matter of profound self-criticism. In fact, you should begin with recognizing your positive qualities and reinforcing them, and only when you have done this should you examine your shortcomings and correct them.

To shorten the distance

Rabbi Jacob Katz offered the following insightful thought in a talk at Yeshivat Netiv Aryeh in the Jewish Quarter of the Old City in Jerusalem:

"This issue is really about the distance between the mind and the heart. We know things on an intellectual level and we can explain what needs to be done and why, but we fail to put it into practice. We do not succeed in drawing it into our hearts. We do not succeed in really feeling it. The Kotzker Rebbe said that the distance between the mind and the heart is greater than the distance between heaven and earth. During this month, the month of Elul, we feel the closeness a little more; the connection between the mind and the heart is a little stronger. At this time of year, there is a greater opportunity to progress. This is the challenge each of us faces in every area of life – to shorten the distance between the mind and the heart, to truly feel what we know is true."

SEPTEMBER 1: BACK TO SCHOOL

We are the teachers

The first of September has arrived, but the optimum period for learning does not start now. In fact, it has just ended. Summer vacation is a transformative time when the most influential and meaningful learning takes place: it is the time when our children receive a real-world education. They watch closely as their parents talk, work, and drive. They see how their parents behave in a park, on a beach, or in a hotel. In short, they absorb the way in which the world outside of school operates.

Before we deposit our children once again into the hands of their teachers (with many thanks to you!), we need to remember that the most significant connection in life is the connection between a parent and child. We hear many lovely stories at this time of year about "the best teacher I had," which are all wonderful and of course, very important, but ultimately it is the parents who are the most influential educators in a child's life. Indeed, it could be said that the manner in which we purchase our children's books, wrap them carefully in a protective book cover, and prepare them for school is just as important as the content of the books themselves.

Almost any kind of connection can be severed. Friendships can be broken, marriage can end in divorce, a contract can be breached – but the bond of parenthood can never be terminated. Even if, throughout life, parents and children are in conflict with one another or don't have the best relationship, what connects them is eternal.

The parental bond is so fundamental and powerful that the Torah uses it as a model for the connection between God and ourselves: "You are children of the Lord, your God." In our relationship with God, even if there is a disconnect, even if we have grown apart, become confused, and lost our way, we will forever remain His children.

"Shalom, Kita Alef"

At a glance, Naomi Shemer's "*Shalom, Kita Alef*" is simply a sweet children's song celebrating the first day of school. However, there is a much deeper message within. "Donna sleeps, Donna wakes up,

Donna folds her pajamas," the song begins. But when it comes to describing the mother's separation from her child, Naomi Shemer turns to the eternal Bible: "And Mother is already standing there, like Yocheved or Miriam in the reeds. The breeze is singing, 'A great journey begins today; *shalom*, first grade.'"

What a powerful image: Moses's mother and sister, two women who built the nation, watch over baby Moses with trepidation, hope, and prayers for the future. So too, with trepidation, hope, and prayers, we accompany our children to the school gate.

This is not only about a pencil case and a backpack, and even the usual threat of a teachers' strike cannot diminish this tradition. We connect ourselves today with all the mothers and fathers of generations before us who supported and looked on with love as the next generation ventured forth and blossomed.

A similar hidden gem is found in the song "You Will Not Defeat Me," in which Naomi Shemer envisions how we will flourish here and never again be vanquished from our land.

She describes looking out the window and seeing "schoolchildren with a satchel on their backs and flowering myrtle branches in their hands."

Our Sages stated: "Jerusalem was destroyed only because schoolchildren stopped learning" (Shabbat 119b). A nation is measured not only by its physical strength; it requires young children learning in school. The nation exists because of them and their learning, and if they are also holding myrtle branches (symbolizing nature and Shabbat), then our enemies will never defeat us.

A great journey begins today. To the more than one million school children who are returning to their studies with their bags on their backs – may you be successful!

Guard the deposit

Copious messages of congratulations, status updates, and heartfelt blessings abound wishing students well at the beginning of a new school year. I have a feeling a great storm would erupt should any minister today choose to share the following letter that was sent to students in 5709 (1949), the first school year after the establishment of the State of Israel. The letter was written by Zalman Shazar, then Minister of Education who would later become the third president of Israel. His letter reads as follows:

"Grow up well, young brothers and sisters. Open your hearts wide to receive the Torah of Israel. Learn of the heavy price that has been paid by generations of your ancestors for their loyalty to our faith, how bitter was the taste of slavery, and of the expectations arising from the vision of the rebirth of Israel. Remember: You have a calling as the successors. The entire historical value of our revival depends on this. Love the legacy of your people. Learn to revive within yourselves the glory of holy aspirations and an eternal mission. Cherish our great creators and teachers, both from ancient times and those living among us today. Connect your hearts and souls with our eternal heritage, ever renewed. May the vision of Israel's prophets be the vision of your future lives. The hope of our nation is the State of Israel; the hope of the State of Israel is our youth. Gather strength, learn well, deepen your knowledge, know the Torah of Israel, cherish the creative human spirit, love freedom. And guard very well the heritage and hope that have been deposited with you."

Amen.

THIRD OF ELUL:
ANNIVERSARY OF THE DEATH OF RAV KOOK
In need of consolation

What do we need above all else? Consolation. On the third of Elul, we mark the passing of Rabbi Avraham Yitzchak HaCohen Kook, the great consoler, who passed away in 5695 (1935). After two thousand years of exile, after being trampled, humiliated, and expelled from many countries, Rav Kook insisted that our generation needs to hear about good things, such as the greatness of our potential, the greatness of our Torah, and the greatness of our shared mission. It seems to me that we are still thirsty for this, for positive, compassionate, and empowering words – in the way we talk to each other, in the way we speak within our families, and within culture and the media.

In the words of Rav Kook: "The consolation of Israel is now our greatest and holiest obligation. To give the gift of true consolation is the obligation of scholars, *tzaddikim*, *kedoshim*, and all those who detect within themselves a heartfelt inclination to walk in the ways of the pious. We have become accustomed to speak nothing but harsh words of rebuke.... We must console...expressing ourselves always in praise of Israel, to speak favorably of Jews, and always find what is good and glorious in them, and by doing so lift their spirits."

Glorious *teshuva*

In the title of his book, *Orot HaTeshuva*, Rav Kook expresses his novel perspective on *teshuva*. He believes that *teshuva* is not gloomy soul-searching over past misdeeds but rather a positive process filled with light. Rav Kook passed away at the beginning of the month of *teshuva*. I have chosen to share a taste of his principles that are appropriate for this time of year:

"The sin of Adam, the first man, was that he was alienated from his essence; he listened to the opinion of the serpent and lost himself. He did not know how to give a clear answer to the question, 'Where are you?' because he did not know his own soul."

"When we forget the essence of our soul, everything becomes mixed up and full of doubt. And so, first and foremost, *teshuva* is about returning to oneself, to the root of one's soul, and then one will immediately return to God, to the Soul of souls... and this holds true whether we are speaking of an individual, an entire nation, all of humanity, or even repairing the whole world. The error always comes from forgetting oneself."

"A foundation of *teshuva* is acknowledgement of responsibility for one's actions, which comes from belief in free will...when one admits that there is no one else to blame for one's sins and their consequences except oneself."

When the soul is beautiful

It is impossible to summarize the multifaceted life and extensive thought of Rabbi Avraham Yitzchak HaCohen Kook; I can only give a small taste of it. Here, for example, is a brief but beautiful thought regarding the soul, about which he wrote prolifically:

"The beauty of the universe is felt in proportion to the beauty found in the innermost part of the soul."

This thought is explained in the book *Mishpatei HaRav Kook*, written by Asaf Fasi: "There are people to whom it is fun to show things because they are easily excited and impressed. They know how to be enthusiastic. With this thought, Rav Kook suggests an additional reason why it is so delightful to share beautiful sights with such people: They do not get excited in an ordinary way because the beauty they see is the beauty within themselves. They are able to see the wonder of the world because their souls are beautiful and wondrous. They are full of gentleness and nobility, and therefore that is what they see outside themselves. The more beautiful one is on the inside, the more one is able to discover the beauty of the world and to love it. The beauty of the world is felt in proportion to the beauty found in the innermost part of the soul."

EIGHTEENTH OF ELUL
What did the Baal Shem Tov reveal?

Mazal tov to *Hasidut* on its birthday today. On the eighteenth of Elul, both the Baal Shem Tov, founder of the hasidic movement, and Rabbi Shneur Zalman of Liadi, founder of Chabad *Hasidut*, were born. How can we even begin to describe their contribution to the Jewish world and the world as a whole?

Elie Wiesel, the Holocaust survivor, author, and Nobel Prize winner, tried to explain the Baal Shem Tov's contribution to the world. In his book *The Hasidic Soul*, Wiesel describes what caused the multitudes to be swept up and follow the Baal Shem Tov three hundred years ago.

"He was the first to tell the desperately poor that they exist because God remembers each and every one of them, that each of them is fulfilling a function in the destiny of his people, in his own way in accordance with his means. The Baal Shem Tov promised that a simple but sincere prayer is accepted. He said that a wagon driver who kisses a Torah scroll brings more joy to God than angels singing His praises, and that pride born from knowledge is worse than ignorance. Man's greatness, he taught them, is found in a humble spirit. One therefore needs to begin by submitting oneself to God. Only in this way can a person grow. The Baal Shem Tov taught that sometimes it is enough to have faith in the existence of a secret, without the definiteness of knowing. Similarly, one does not need much in order to be elevated and find fulfillment. He explained that one tear or one prayer can change the course of events. A short melodic tune may contain all the joy in the world, and when it is heard, it may well change our fate. No elite group has a monopoly on songs and tears. He taught how to fight sadness by means of joy, and revealed a secret: sadness flows from looking only at oneself, while joy arrives the moment we open our eyes to look at the creation and the people around us."

The heart of the Tanya

The founder of the Chabad hasidic movement, Rabbi Shneur Zalman of Liadi, developed an approach that has influenced the Jewish world to this day. Given our current state of affairs, it seems to me that it is more vital and relevant than ever before. His book, known as "the Tanya," lays out the principles of his approach, with chapter 32 considered by many to be the most fundamental chapter. (Note: Each Hebrew letter has a numerical value, so that chapter 32 is *lamed* [30] *bet* [2]. "*Lamed bet*" also spells "*lev*," meaning heart). Here are some of the principles contained within the chapter:

"On account of their common root in the One God, all of Israel are called brothers; only their bodies are separate." In the root of our souls, all of us come from the same source. We are brothers and sisters. Externally, we look different and separate, but there is a common factor that unites us all.

"The foundation and purpose of the entire Torah is to elevate and exalt the soul high above the body." Everything is encompassed within the struggle between the soul and the body, between the spiritual and the material, between what is right to do and what the ego and self-interest tell us to do. Our task in life is to train the soul to lead the body, and not the other way around.

And what do we do in the face of someone who seems wicked, misled, and harmful? "Abhor the bad side of them and love the good that is hidden inside them, for this is the divine spark that can revive the divine soul." We need to hate the bad, but always remember that there is a spark of goodness in every-one – and to love that spark.

Tishrei

ROSH HASHANA
The sound of the soul

The Hebrew year begins with a two-day festival on the first and second of Tishrei. These two days herald the beginning of the Ten Days of Repentance, which conclude on Yom Kippur. More than the custom of dipping an apple in honey, or eating pomegranate seeds, or taking a bite from the head of a fish, the principal mitzva of Rosh HaShana is hearing the shofar: "It shall be a day of trumpet blasts for you."

Other nations celebrate the new year with a huge party. They go out into the streets and gather in the city center, where a noisy countdown is heard as the last seconds of the old year tick away. We start the new year in a completely different manner. After yet another year of fluff and chatter, a few moments are devoted to being quiet and just listening. Before the mitzva of hearing the various shofar sounds – *tekia* (one long blast), *shevarim* (three broken sounds), *terua* (nine staccato notes) – we recite an unusual blessing: "Blessed are You, Lord of the universe, who has sanctified us with His commandments and commanded us to hear the sound of the shofar." We bless before partaking of a mitzva that does not involve doing anything, only listening.

The sound of the shofar evokes important events in our history: the Akeda, when a ram was sacrificed in place of Isaac; the blasts of the shofar that were heard at the giving of the Torah at Mount Sinai; the Jubilee year when slaves were set free, announced by the blowing of a shofar. It also reminds us of the future redemption which, according to the prophets, will be ushered in with the sounds of the shofar.

For several moments, we do not speak, react, or argue. We just listen. We do not jump in and express our opinion; we quiet the noise and escape the hustle and bustle all around us. We do this in order to hear a pure and simple voice – the voice of the soul.

Which Reuben will you be?

Have you, by any chance, spent time this Rosh HaShana imagining what you will be like next Rosh HaShana? There is a view that this is really what our focus should be. Rather than examining the year gone by, we should primarily look forward to the coming year and consider exactly what we want from ourselves in every area of life.

This interesting and practical suggestion was offered by Rabbi Kalonymus Kalman Shapira, the Rebbe of Piaseczno. He was murdered during the Holocaust but left a wonderful educational legacy. He suggests that as we look ahead to the next Rosh HaShana, we envision how we would like to be, and then examine what we need to do in order to achieve that:

"If you desire to serve Hashem and to elevate yourself, and not to be in the same place at the age of seventy as you were on your bar mitzva, do this: Every year, set a goal for yourself. If your name is Reuben, for example, imagine the Reuben you would like to be a year from now – his achievements, his work, his character traits, and everything else about him. With this imaginary Reuben in mind, measure yourself against him throughout the year so that you can see where you are falling short and what kind of work you need to do to become him. Strive so that your service of God and personal refinement on a daily basis will be sufficient to meet the goal – one year from now – of becoming the Reuben you wish to be."

The best *siman* of all

The *simanim* (symbols) are a central part of the dinner table on Rosh HaShana. We dip an apple in honey and wish for a year that will be as sweet as honey. We eat a pomegranate, praying that our merits will be as many as the seeds of this fruit. During the Rosh HaShana meal in the home of Rabbi Yisrael Meir HaCohen of Radin, known as the Chafetz Chaim, the rabbi spoke to his guests about the most important *siman*, one that is useful even during times of tension and distress:

"We know there is significance and strength in the symbolic foods we prepare for Rosh HaShana, and we therefore strive to eat what is sweet, and to bless and pray over these foods. But if we are so particular in looking for meaningful *simanim*, there are none better than a pleasant disposition, a smile, and the patience we show to others. And there are no worse *simanim* than anger and intransigence. After all, our behavior has influence and consequences too, as is written in the Gemara: 'Whoever shows compassion to others is granted compassion from Heaven' (Shabbat 151b). On Rosh HaShana we need to pay special attention to the *simanim* of affection, love, and warmheartedness."

Sheheḥeyanu (who has given us life)

"Shalom Sivan, this is Hagit Rhein from Karnei Shomron. On the eve of Rosh HaShana 5767 (2007), I was preparing to light the holiday candles. This was a month and a half after my son, Benaya Rhein, fell in the Second Lebanon War. As we light the holiday candles, we are supposed to bless, "Who has given us life, sustained us, and enabled us to reach this occasion." I stood in front of the candles and felt that I could not sincerely offer this blessing. I wanted the blessing to come from my heart, but I felt that saying it this time would be fake. How could I utter the words, "Who has given us life" when my son had just recently been killed? I stood in front of the candles with tears in my eyes. I prayed that I would somehow gather the strength to bless with joy.

"After what seemed like an eternity, I suddenly looked around me. I saw our seven children, our sons-in-law, our daughters-in-law, our beautiful grandchildren, and suddenly I understood: Yes – "Who has given us life"! Say thank you for all that you have, for the enormous abundance in your life that cannot be taken for granted. I felt my heart open and I gave a shout: "Who has given us life, sustained us, and allowed us to reach this occasion!" I think they must have heard me all the way to Qalqilya. . . I have tried hard to hold on to the insight from that moment and to adopt it as a general perspective on life. May we all succeed in lifting ourselves this year, to be thankful for what we have, to see the good within whatever challenges arise, and to rejoice that we have been sustained to reach this occasion."

We are all standing

How do we approach the new year? We can find guidance in the first passage in the Torah portion of *Nitzavim* that we read at this time: "You are all standing today before the Lord your God – the leaders of your tribes, your elders and your officers, every man of Israel, your young children, your women, and your convert who is within your camp, both your woodcutters and water-drawers."

First and foremost, we approach the new year together: "You are all standing today." The leaders and the elders, the women and the children, woodcutters and water-drawers. Both the elite and the common folk, all the sectors and various communities ultimately share in the same story. We cannot run away from the unity that is ingrained within us.

But this is not enough. There are those who say that this passage does not only speak about the nation, but about aspects of the human character and experience. On Rosh HaShana, we carry with us those moments during the past year in which we were "leaders of your tribes," moments of success when we were at our peak, and also periods in which we were "woodcutters and water-drawers," when we were not as strong due to our struggles.

During the days of *teshuva*, we gain insight as we look back at all our experiences in the previous year, and in doing so, we are all "standing before the Lord your God," with a prayer for a good and sweet year.

THIRD OF TISHREI: FAST OF GEDALIA
Why do we fast?

This is a fast with low ratings, if you will excuse the expression. Perhaps it is because of the date (coming after two days of a holiday), and perhaps also because of the reason for the fast – it is easier to fast because of something our enemies did to us than it is to fast because of something that we did to ourselves.

After the destruction of the First Temple, the kingdom of Babylonia sent most of the Jews living in the Land of Israel into exile. However, a small minority of Jews remained. Gedalia ben Ahikam was appointed governor over this little group, but he was murdered by his fellow Jews under the leadership of Yishmael ben Netanya. The king of Ammon had sent Yishmael ben Netanya on this mission, and there are those who say that Yishmael saw himself as more deserving of governorship than Gedalia. This was a power struggle between Jews, but the tragedy was that, at this point, barely any power had been left to them. There was nothing more than a glowing ember, but even so, they were determined to fight over that ember until it too was extinguished.

Gedalia's loyalists warned of the plot to kill him, but he refused to believe it could happen. His murder symbolized the absolute end of Jewish community life in the Land of Israel during that period, something unheard of since the days of Yehoshua bin Nun. The handful of Jews who were still in the land scattered. For seventy years, until the return to Zion and the building of the Second Temple, no Jewish sovereignty existed in the Land of Israel.

Our fast days do not exist simply to commemorate events of the past. Rather, they prompt us to learn the lessons of the past in order to improve our present and secure our future.

TEN DAYS OF TESHUVA
תשוב"ה (*Teshuva*)

The first ten days of the year are called the Ten Days of *Teshuva* (repentance). Maimonides writes of these special days in *Mishneh Torah, Hilkhot Teshuva* 2:6: "Even though *teshuva* and crying out to Hashem are always timely and will be accepted throughout the year, during the ten days between Rosh HaShana and Yom Kippur, *teshuva* is particularly welcome and atonement is immediately granted, as it is said (Is. 55:6), 'Seek Hashem where He is to be found; call out to Him when He is near.'" Now He is near.

So how do we do *teshuva*? How do we even begin such a personal and introspective process? In the first days of the hasidic movement, Reb Zusha of Anipoli heard a profound explanation about the meaning of *teshuva*. He then said that he could not reach such a high level, and therefore he would divide *teshuva* into smaller parts, based on the letters of the word. The division he made was as follows:

- ת: *Tav* – Wholehearted (*tamim*) you shall be with Hashem your God.

- ש: *Shin* – I have placed (*shiviti*) Hashem before me always.

- ו: *Vav* – You shall love (*ve'ahavta*) your neighbor as yourself.

- ב: *Bet* – In all (*bekhol*) your ways you shall know Him.

- ה: *Heh* – Humbly (**hatznea**) walk with your God.

Wholeheartedness, devotion, love of fellow Jews, love for Hashem, humility – Reb Zusha offers us five paths to *teshuva*, and in doing so he brings *teshuva* closer to us and makes it more accessible.

Perhaps there is more to the approach of five paths to *teshuva*. Reb Zusha might be showing us that there are different ways of bringing about change and improvement on a personal basis. We do not need to be alarmed, perhaps imagining that a challenge is too daunting for us to undertake. It is possible, necessary even, for every individual to find their own path.

In the same spirit, it is told that Reb Zusha was accustomed to say: "I am not afraid that they will ask me in heaven after I die why I wasn't like Moses. I am not afraid that they will ask me why I wasn't like Maimonides. I am only afraid that they will ask me why I wasn't Zusha."

Everyone needs to find his own path, to strive to be the best version of himself.

A pause for thought

We need to pay attention to our prayers during the Ten Days of *Teshuva* so that we notice the changes that are made in the *Amida*. From Rosh HaShana until Yom Kippur, we substitute "the holy King" for "the holy God" in this prayer, as well as "the King of judgment" for the usual "King who loves righteousness and justice." In addition, there are four insertions in the *Amida*: (1) "Remember us for life, King who desires life; inscribe us in the Book of Life, for Your sake, O living God," (2) "Who is like You, merciful

Father, who in compassion remembers His creatures for life," (3) "Inscribe all the children of Your covenant for a good life," and finally, (4) "And in the Book of Life, blessing, peace, and prosperity, deliverance, consolation, and favorable decrees, may we and all Your people, the House of Israel, be remembered and inscribed before You for a good life and for peace."

The guiding words here are King, life, and compassion, which together constitute the essence of this period.

But it is not only the inspiring content of alternative words and requests that distinguishes the *Amida* during the Ten Days of *Teshuva*. It is the awareness that accompanies them that makes such a profound difference in our prayer. Those who run through the *Amida* by heart througout the year must stop for a few moments and pay special attention to what they are saying. Invariably, they will relate to the prayers differently, with more focus. We are not completely changing the *Amida*, just refreshing it for a few days. Perhaps this is really the purpose of these ten days: to reexamine the familiar and to make tiny, manageable changes. Revolutionary changes are certainly welcome at this time of year – or any other time – but small changes in our daily routine can make a big difference.

Optimism is in the air

How do we feel during the first days of the year? Netanel Peretz, an educator from Ashdod, beautifully described our feelings as follows:

"Aside from the blessings and hopes that are showered upon us this week, I would like to add a little something. I have noticed that every year at this time, a small miracle happens. We all succeed during several specific days to return to ourselves and believe that change is possible. This is literally a miracle. Even the most desperate and broken spirits manage to push aside the enveloping darkness of their daily lives and open a small window. At this time of year, you suddenly see millions of people inspired with the belief that this year will be beautiful and different. That they will be better. That their hearts will be more prepared and open to receiving the goodness that is continuously showered upon them from above. That perhaps this year, they will have the courage to walk this difficult path without fear. That they will have the strength to make amends.

"Suddenly, something softens, if only briefly, as many decide to let go for a moment and give change a chance, believing change is possible.

"And I thought to myself that this cannot be taken for granted, this ability to return to ourselves and believe in the possibility of change for the better. I thought about how appropriate it is to be thankful for this miracle that happens at the beginning of every Tishrei. Let the blessings of the new year begin to flow."

More than a glass of milk

While shopping in a kosher grocery store in Manchester, England, I happened to see a pamphlet entitled *Torat Avigdor*, containing insights from the educator and lecturer Avigdor Miller. I opened it and read the following:

"During these days, people focus their attention on their sins – especially the big ones – as they examine their deeds of the past year. However, sometimes our greatest sin is not smiling at another person. Whoever gives a smile to a poor person gives him a lot more than money. Whoever uses hurtful words to upset another person causes more pain than if he had stolen the same person's money. Whoever causes another to feel good, to feel joy, tranquility, and a sense of self-worth – that is the highest form of giving. How many times could we have said a good word to a friend, our spouse, or our children, but we missed the chance? We need to think for a moment before we enter our house, to stop when our hand is on the doorknob, and plan the kind words we will say to those at home. It is so easy to do.

"People walk in the street with sour faces and think that this is okay. Yet it is written in *Pirkei Avot* 1:15: 'Greet every person with a cheerful countenance.' Moreover, our Sages stated: 'It is better to show white teeth to a friend than to give him milk to drink' (Ketubot 111b). Imagine someone who has worked hard all day, is walking down the street, thirsty, and then receives a glass of cold milk from us. It's wonderful. But offering him a smile ('whitening his teeth') satisfies a much greater thirst. This is an important part of our work as we approach Yom Kippur, and it is so accessible and easy to do."

To believe in human greatness

During the 1970s, the profound educator Rabbi Shlomo Wolbe was asked to explain the essence of *teshuva* to a group of high school students. This is what he said:

"If I were to be asked what I believe in, I would say: 'I believe in the greatness of man!' And within that greatness is the capacity to correct ourselves, our environment, and the entire world. Many people believe in God. This is not unusual. But not everyone believes in the greatness of the human being. I believe. I believe that a human being can have a living relationship with his Creator, that a human being can do great and wonderful things not only outwardly, but also within, and that he has awesome spiritual strength to take control of himself and harness his magnificent transformative power."

This is Rabbi Wolbe's message for us as we strive for self-correction during the Ten Days of *Teshuva*: to believe not only in the greatness of God, but in our own greatness, too.

A small resolution

During the Ten Days of *Teshuva* between Rosh HaShana and Yom Kippur, it is customary to make a resolution to better ourselves. We should try to make one resolution for improvement in a specific area of our lives and stick by it. This can be any small, positive change – in relation to ourselves, family, community, *tzedaka*, prayer, learning, reducing time spent on the internet, and so on. In this way, we can ensure that the promises we made to ourselves at the beginning of the year are not forgotten. One small resolution can endure as we strive to fulfill our promises in the days ahead.

There are those who say that a new year's resolution is like a new garment that is acquired for the soul. The resolution needs to be practical and achievable. In his youth, Rabbi Sholom Schwardon, an inspirational speaker known as the Maggid of Jerusalem, approached his rabbi at the beginning of the year and asked which worthwhile resolution he should adopt. The rabbi answered, "Think carefully and choose a resolution that you are sure you can keep throughout the year." He returned to his rabbi with his choice and the rabbi said, "Now cut this resolution in two and take upon yourself only half of it in order to ensure your success."

YOM KIPPUR

Happy Yom Kippur!

Yom Kippur on the tenth of Tishrei is considered the holiest and most important day in the Jewish year. In the Torah it is written: "Because on this day, there will be atonement for you, to purify you from all your sins; before God you will be cleansed" (Lev. 16:30). This is the day on which Moses came down from Mount Sinai with the second set of Tablets of the Covenant, having broken the first set when he saw the sin of the Golden Calf. Yom Kippur commemorates the day that the children of Israel were given a second chance with the second set of Tablets, and so it became a day of atonement and forgiveness throughout the generations.

Here is something to which we do not pay sufficient attention: It's clear that the mitzva on Yom Kippur is to fast, but what about the mitzva on the day before Yom Kippur – the mitzva to eat? This is a mitzva in its own right, and not just to help us feel less hungry during the fast on Yom Kippur. Our Sages tell us that the idea of Yom Kippur is so great that it is actually deserving of a joyful feast. Of course, it is impossible to celebrate the day in that manner, as it is a fast day, so we bring the feast forward to the day before, the eve of Yom Kippur. The Spanish commentator Rabbeinu Yona of Girondi, who lived around eight hundred years ago, wrote the following: "And because of the fast on Yom Kippur, we are obliged to partake of the feast that is held to rejoice in the mitzva on Yom Kippur eve."

But just a moment. Why are we rejoicing with a feast? What are we so happy about? We rejoice about the very existence of Yom Kippur, a day of appeasement and atonement. It is a day that brings with it the capacity to change, the possibility to forgive and erase, to begin anew and rebuild from crisis – a day that is a reminder that human beings have free choice. For all of these reasons, when we look deeply into the substance of this special day, it really is appropriate to wish each other a happy Yom Kippur.

The wonder of *teshuva*

Rabbi Jacob Edelstein, of blessed memory, was the rabbi of Ramat HaSharon. We were privileged to live there and get to know him well. Here are some of his pearls of wisdom regarding Yom Kippur:

"How is it possible to erase things that a person has done? What good is regret? Does it make sins disappear? If a person eats something that causes a stomachache, and afterward, he's sorry he ate it, will regret benefit his stomach now? The process of *teshuva* is higher than our minds can grasp. It is beyond nature. It is one of the wonders of creation, one of the greatest gifts we have received – the possibility to start over again."

"There is a wonderful passage that reveals a secret to us: 'Return, Israel, to Hashem your God.' In other words, a person must return to Hashem. If this was an ascent to a new place or moving to somewhere different, it would not say 'return.' From this we learn that *teshuva* means going back to our true origins. The meaning of *teshuva* is not to change, but to return to our proper place, to be who we are supposed to be."

"Someone once said that in his youth, he wanted to change the world. He later saw that this was difficult and decided to change only the people in his country. Then he decided to at least change the residents of his city. When he failed, he tried to just change the members of his family. Finally, he understood that he must first change himself. And then, after he worked on changing himself, he saw that he slowly began to influence his family, his city, his country, and the entire world. Improving the world starts with self-improvement. Our desire is for wholesale, widespread change, but such change begins with character refinement on the part of each and every individual."

A second *Kol Nidrei*

Israeli journalist Moshe Erlanger relates the following story:

"Several years ago, I was compelled at the last minute to spend Yom Kippur in Frankfurt, Germany. I rented a room in a hotel near the main synagogue in Frankfurt, put together a pre-fast meal, and went to pray with a feeling of longing for Israel and regret for what I would be missing there.

"I found that the main synagogue was a magnificent building with two thousand congregants in attendance, the majority of whom did not pray there during the year. The cantor, Tzadok Greenwald, began the *Kol Nidrei* service, and the passion and emotion in his prayer were evident. He choked as his voice broke, then rose and fell. The entire crowd was moved together with him.

"At the conclusion of the service, I approached the cantor and asked him why he became so emotional during the *Kol Nidrei* service. This was his answer:

"'For many years, I have been the cantor here during the High Holy Days. As a descendant of Holocaust survivors, it is a great privilege to be a cantor, particularly here in this wretched land. Several years ago, I had an extraordinary encounter as I was leaving the synagogue at the end of Yom Kippur. The last of the crowd had already gone home to break the fast. The *gabbai* (synagogue manager) had locked the main gate and I was leaving through a side door, tired and hungry. Near the main gate, I saw an elderly man wearing a white *kippa*. He turned to me and asked, "Why are the gates of the synagogue locked? When does *Kol Nidrei* begin? Please, answer me. Why are the gates locked?" I was silent. My heart was breaking. "My dear friend, listen to me. *Kol Nidrei* was last night. Yom Kippur was today," I stammered. "The crowd has gone home. *Kol Nidrei* will come again next year." The man grabbed my hands and began to cry like a little boy. "I have never missed *Kol Nidrei*. I promised my father, may his memory be blessed, that I would go every year to hear *Kol Nidrei* in a synagogue. This is the only connection I have with my father, and it is the only connection I have with my *Yiddishkeit*."

"'I knew what I had to do. "My dear friend, you missed nothing," I told him. "I am the chief cantor of this synagogue. Come with me to hear *Kol Nidrei*." I opened the side door, sat him down in a chair, gave him a prayer book, and wrapped myself in a tallit. I began to recite *Kol Nidrei*. This was the most powerful prayer I had ever prayed in my life. Thousands of empty chairs and just me, the elderly man, and the Holy One, blessed be He. I forgot about the fast. I was focused only on the connection between a disconnected Jew and his father, which may just as well have been the connection between me and my father – that is, our Father in heaven.

"'I never saw the man again, but every time I pray *Kol Nidrei,* I think about him and a million other Jews like him. I think also about the side door – the open door through which anyone, in the end, can enter.'"

Only this moment

What do we do when we face a challenge – for example, a long day of prayers in the synagogue? How do we maintain our concentration? Rabbi Nachman of Breslov recommends that we focus just on the present moment:

"The most useful advice when it comes to serving Hashem, may He be blessed, is to imagine – each and every day – that you have that day alone to serve Him. Even better would be to imagine that, while praying, you have no more than that hour to do so. You need only think about this day and this moment. When you want to truly serve Hashem, it may seem to be a heavy burden that is impossible to bear, but if you think that all you have is today, it will not be a burden at all. Because you have nothing in this world except this day and this hour, and tomorrow is another world completely."

This advice is appropriate not only for Yom Kippur, but for every major challenge that we face. Divide it into manageable portions and try to focus only on the present moment and the matter immediately at hand. Be exclusively in that moment; experience it completely, without indulging thoughts of the past or the future.

I am a loser

Not all of us can be "the best." In life, there is not only victory, but considerable failure too. We may ask what defines failure and what defines victory – being number one? If you are number two, or ten, are you then worthless? Once a year, the twenty-five hours of Yom Kippur bring us a different awareness. Rabbi Chaim Navon wrote about this contrast for the Shimshoni congregation in the city of Modi'in prior to Yom Kippur:

"People say, 'No one knows the name of Bar Kokhba's second-in-command.' I happen to know it: they called him Yehoshua ben Galgula. Yet even if we did not know his name, so what? Once an interviewer asked me, 'How would you want the world to remember you in a hundred years?' I answered him, 'The world will not remember me in a hundred years. I hope that my great-grandchildren will remember me with affection and appreciation, and this is the most someone like me can hope for.'

"I believe that I will merit appreciation from my great-grandchildren not because I was a 'winner,' but because they will know that I struggled honorably with the challenges that life brought my way, including the times that I failed. You cannot enter the spirit of Yom Kippur if you think of yourself as a winner. The High Priest himself removed his majestic gold vestments on Yom Kippur and wore simple white vestments instead. On Yom Kippur we have the courage to say 'Sometimes we are imperfect.'"

YOM KIPPUR PRAYERS
Kol Nidrei

Three Torah scrolls are removed from the holy ark and the entire congregation declares that all their vows, oaths, and promises are null and void and no longer exist.

Composer and singer Kobi Oz wrote the following: "On the High Holy Days, we peel off the heavy armor that we have worn all year, our 'show-off armor,' and try to reinvent ourselves. The High Holy Days whisper to us: This is not you – you are not a singer, a four-eyes with thick glasses, a Tunisian-Moroccan, a Sderoti (someone from Sderot), a Tel Avivi, a bodybuilder, a weakling, the son of Jojo, of blessed memory, or the son of Raymonde, may she live, husband of Batsheva, and on and on. All these definitions are not really you."

Vidui (confession)

אשמנו (We have transgressed), בגדנו (we have betrayed), גזלנו (we have robbed), דברנו דופי (we have slandered), and so on – a sin for every letter of the Hebrew alphabet, from *alef* to *tav*. Ten times in the course of the day, we say *vidui*, in which there is a long list of sins, flaws, and missed opportunities. Afterward, we declare again and again, "For the sin that we have committed before You." Here too is an all-encompassing list, and it is also arranged in alphabetical order. It includes thoughts ("For the sin we have committed before You through improper thoughts"), treatment of others ("For the sin we have committed before You through *lashon hara*" [gossip or insulting speech about another person]), hatred of others for no reason ("For the sin we have committed before You through baseless hatred"), business transactions ("For the sin we have committed before You through improper business dealings"), and sins committed in many other areas of our lives.

In a culture where the message broadcast daily is "you owe it to yourself" and "just do it," it is not customary to examine our actions and admit that we often make mistakes. The jurist, Professor Yedidya Stern, notes that every day of the year, we engage in "lawyering." Everything is measured in terms of the law: Is this legal or illegal? And if someone is not convicted, then he must be completely innocent. "Yom Kippur presents a completely different picture," he says. "The one who prays does not try to find a good lawyer who can fool the judge, but instead tries to take responsibility. He conducts the trial himself, with a sincere and intense internal investigation."

Seder HaAvoda (**Temple service led by the High Priest**)

Thanks to the singer Ishay Ribo and his wonderful song, "*Seder HaAvoda*," many people have understood for the first time what

used to take place at the holiest time of the year in the most hallowed place of all. The *Seder HaAvoda* is the central part of the
Musaf prayer on Yom Kippur, and it describes the service led by
the holy priest in the Holy Temple on this day.

Are you familiar with the term "scapegoat?" Its source is here,
on Yom Kippur. Two goats were chosen, one to be sacrificed in
the Holy Temple, the other to be sent into the desert.

Two hundred years ago in Germany, Rabbi Samson Raphael
Hirsch suggested that these represent the two options we face:
the desert or holiness. "In a world of natural forces lacking freedom, the human being alone has freedom. This freedom holds the
option of doing the will of Hashem or opposing it. A person can
be a goat in the desert or a goat that serves Hashem – the choice
is his. A person decides where he wishes to go, to the desert or
to a place of holiness, and he can make this choice at any time.
However, there is no value in choosing holiness if the option to go
the way of the desert is not also available. And by the same token,
choosing the desert does not disgrace a person unless he could
just as equally choose the path to holiness. The elevated status of
human beings depends on having the choice to sin, and honor is
achieved by obeying the will of Hashem when we have the ability
to do otherwise. Moral virtue is expressed when people choose
what is good."

Grant honor to Your people

"And so, Lord our God, grant honor to Your people, glory to those
who fear You, hope to those who seek You, confident speech to
those who yearn for You."

Hold on – why are we continually asking for honor and
glory during the prayers of the High Holy Days? Because of our
ego? Do we want to become an empire?

I recently looked at the division of the world population
according to religion. There are 2.3 billion Christians in the world,

constituting 30 percent of the global population. Muslims comprise 24 percent of the population, 16 percent have no religion, 15 percent are Hindus, 7 percent are Buddhists, and in a tiny slice barely visible on the graph is the Jewish population: 14 million, just about 0.02 percent. That's it. Given our tiny percentage, it is hard to believe the tremendous level of energy and passion that is directed toward us, both out of love and hate.

Our strength is not in quantity, but in quality. We are not in a physical competition with anyone, because we will not win. We do not pray for the honor of being the strongest. Rather, we pray for our worldview to be respected, for our truth to be recognized and valued. It is not just the world's understanding of the State of Israel. The war on BDS is just the beginning. From here we can be an inspiration to the whole world. The message of *teshuva* on Yom Kippur and man's ability to make amends is more relevant than ever in this age of doubt and depression, not to mention Shabbat and its revolutionary message of rest for the fast-paced world in which we live.

In light of this, Rav Kook wrote the following:

"We need to instill in ourselves that the goal of Israeli nationalism is not to show off our strength or conquer nations. Such is the desire of some nations due to their enormous self-love. The goal of our nationalism should be to bring blessing and perfection to the entire world because of our love for the human race."

Ne'ila (closing prayer, literally, "locking")

"Awesome God, grant us pardon in the closing hour."

Ne'ila is the prayer that seals the holiest day of the year. "Open a gate for us at the moment the gate is closing, because this day is over."

Rabbi Avinadav Abukarat once described the following to the Avnei HaḤoshen congregation in Givat Shmuel on Yom Kippur:

"We are still near the start of the school year. I noticed that in kindergarten, each time a father or mother wants to leave, their child stubbornly holds onto a piece of their clothing and refuses to let go. Even though the child knows that in the end his father will leave, he persists anyway and won't let go. Why does he do this? What's the point? He holds on because he wants to grab just one more moment with his father. One more moment of closeness, one more hug of warmth and connection. It seems to me that this is what we are doing now during the *Ne'ila* prayer. We ask for one more moment of prayer and holiness. We are grabbing one more minute of the High Holy Days before returning to the ordinary routine of our lives."

SUKKOT

More than Yom Kippur

Five days after Yom Kippur, the festival of Sukkot arrives – days of sitting in a sukka, shaking the lulav, saying special prayers, and an abundance of traditions. We typically think that the climax of the holidays is reached on Yom Kippur during the *Ne'ila* prayer, but our commentators suggest otherwise.

To fast a full day like angels is not the peak experience. There is something much higher, and we call it Sukkot. Yes, this festival with the wooden boards and nails, the sheets and the branches, is a reminder of the booths in which we lived in the desert after we left Egypt. In the Torah it is written, "For seven days you shall live in booths. Every resident among the Israelites shall live in booths, in order that your future generations should know that I had the children of Israel live in booths when I took them out of the land of Egypt" (Lev. 23:42–43).

Yom Kippur lasts for only one day of the year. It is a day of complete cessation of all activity. The purpose of Yom Kippur is to gather strength for all the other days of the year, to incorporate what we receive from this special day into our lives, into all our worldly endeavors. Rav Kook said of this time of year, "The days between Yom Kippur and Sukkot were given for guidance in returning to the matters of this world."

In his eyes, it is as if we are coming down from the World to Come, from Yom Kippur, from the highest heights, to this mundane world of daily living. Now we are asked to take a hammer and nails and build a sukka, to go to the market and buy the four species (lulav, etrog, myrtle, and willow), and to prepare the meals for the festival. But all of this may be done with the uplifting spirit that remains with us from Yom Kippur.

A week of liberation

Each year, just before Sukkot, I am reminded of some of the first words of Torah I ever heard. I was fifteen, and I was attending an educational meeting for young people in Jerusalem. As we were about to eat, a girl named Daphna declared that "we can't sit here and eat without a *devar Torah* (a thought from the Torah), even if it's just something short." I did not know what a "*devar Torah*" was, but she immediately continued. "There is a clear connection between Sukkot and Passover. Both of these festivals teach us to appreciate the most basic necessities of life. On Passover, we learn to appreciate bread after a whole week without it, and on Sukkot, we learn to appreciate our homes after a week of living in booths."

This simple thought stayed with me for years. Rabbi Adin Steinsaltz, a recipient of the Israel Prize, was one of the great leaders of Torah, Talmud, and Hasidism in our generation. He adds depth to the idea that Daphna shared: "In a life that is too settled and fixed, there is a danger of complacency, of an exaggerated sense of security. People and nations who feel too self-satisfied in their present situation can find themselves on the edge of an abyss. The sukka jolts us out of our comfortable existence, takes us away from the stability of our homes, and instills within us a feeling of transience. The sukka liberates us from the feeling that 'I deserve this' and that things are 'mine,' feelings based on superficial perceptions. Instead, we live in the sukka for an entire week with the sense that everything in life is, in fact, temporary."

Sukkot during the Yom Kippur War

The Yom Kippur War was also a Sukkot war. The fighting began on the holy fast day but continued throughout the holiday of Sukkot and long after. Hundreds of soldiers on the northern and southern fronts found themselves, to their great disappointment, without the four species (lulav, etrog, myrtle, and willow), without festival prayer books, without Torah scrolls and, in particular, without a sukka. Rabbi Yeshayahu Hadari, head of Yeshivat HaKotel for three decades, told the following story to a gathering of soldiers commemorating forty years since Sukkot 5734 (1973):

"On a Tuesday evening at the Suez Canal, the tension was enormous. The troops had just endured two days of fierce fighting, heavy casualties, and fear of enemy attacks. The division commander, Avraham Baram, briefed his soldiers before battle and after he concluded the orders, called out: 'Is everything clear? Are there any questions?' Yitzchak Tzefatman, a soldier who had been learning at Yeshivat HaKotel, stood up and said, 'Tomorrow is Erev Sukkot and we ask that you do whatever you can to get us the four species.' After the war, the commanding officer, who described himself as distant from Torah and mitzvot, said that if the ground beneath him had opened up and swallowed him, he would have been less surprised than he was by this strange request. The four species in the middle of a war? But Tzefatman stubbornly insisted, and so, when the officer communicated his requests for supplies that evening, he added, 'And make sure you send the four species.' Initially, he was laughed at over the two-way radio, but eventually they were persuaded to carry out his request. The following morning, the four species arrived. Tzefatman encouraged the officer to hold the four species and recite the blessing, and told him that his mitzva would be in the soldiers' merit and lead to their ultimate victory.

"A year later, on Erev Sukkot, Tzefatman took a brief leave from the yeshiva to buy the four species and travel to the home of the officer, who lived in Holon near Tel Aviv. Together with the lulav, etrog, myrtle, and willow, he gave the officer a book written by Yigal Yadin, whose archaeological findings were starting to be published at this time. Former IDF Chief of Staff Yadin had discovered an ancient letter written by Bar Kokhba, the chief of staff long ago during the rebellion against Rome. Sukkot was approaching as they fought in the campaign, and in his letter, addressed to Yehuda Bar Menashe, Bar Kokhba requested a delivery of the four species. Bar Kokhba wrote that he was sending two of his donkeys to the Ein Gedi region in order to load them with the four species for all the soldiers in his camp. Tzefatman wanted to show his officer that he was not the first to worry about the mitzva of the four species in the midst of battle. Bar Kokhba preceded him by two thousand years! He too had thought about this mitzva and made every effort to observe it, even at the height of a war."

To give

Sukkot is called "the time of our rejoicing," and it is supposed to be an especially happy festival. When we check to see where the word *simḥa* (joy/happiness) appears in the Torah, we discover a fascinating phenomenon. *Simḥa* nearly always appears as a reminder to give to another, to share our personal joy with someone else.

For example, take the song "*VeSamaḥta BeḤagekha*" ("And You Shall Rejoice in Your Festival"). Unfortunately, no one has yet composed music for the continuation of this Torah passage: "And you shall rejoice in your festival – you, and your son, and your daughter, and your manservant, and your maidservant, and the Levite, and the stranger, and the orphan, and the widow, who are within your cities" (Deut. 16:14). Another example of *simḥa* shared with others is found in Deuteronomy 12:18: "You shall eat them before the Lord, your God...you, your son, your daughter, your manservant, your maidservant, and the Levite who is in your cities. And you shall rejoice before the Lord your God in all your endeavors."

Rejoicing occurs together with the family, the servant, the widow, the stranger, the orphan, and the poor. Happiness takes us beyond our self-absorption and focuses on the collective, inherent in which is the inclination to give to others rather than take for oneself.

Celebrating the journey

What exactly do we celebrate on Sukkot? On Passover, we commemorate the Exodus from Egypt, Shavuot celebrates the giving of the Torah, and Yom Kippur is a day of forgiveness. We are accustomed to seeing a "headline" for every holiday. But what is Sukkot's headline? Did something special happen on this festival? "You shall live in booths for seven days," the Torah tells us, "in order that your future generations should know that I had the children of Israel live in booths when I took them out of the land of Egypt" (Lev. 23:42–43).

Sukkot does not celebrate a specific event; it commemorates a forty-year journey, reminding us of an entire generation that wandered in the wilderness. Lawyer Rav Yitzchak Barth from Gush Etzion described the meaning of Sukkot in this way: "Sukkot reminds us not only to celebrate achieving a goal. We do not only commemorate the high points in history, such as the Exodus from Egypt or our entry into the Land of Israel. We also remember the long years of wandering, the gray but equally important years it took to reach our goal."

As we celebrate reaching our destination, we should honor the steps and the efforts that led us there. Indeed, most of our lives are spent on the journey.

Family time

Sukkot is distinguished from other festivals as "our time of joy," but it is also "our family time." My mother-in-law, family guidance counselor Ziva Meir, shared these thoughts:

"Many parents ask, 'Where do I draw the line between time devoted to myself and time devoted to my children?' There is a misunderstanding in the question, however, as the time we devote to our children is, in its very essence, meaningful time devoted to ourselves. There is nothing more wonderful than this. If we regard family time as servitude and sacrifice, then we are missing something. Those who feel enslaved to their children are not doing it right. The most worthwhile self-development comes from within the family unit. This is the best workshop for personal growth. If we are truly connected to ourselves, we will find time for parents, siblings, children, and spouses without a sense of guilt and the feeling that we are constantly losing or missing out. True, things can get complicated during holiday periods, but equating personal time with family time should be our guiding principle. There once was a girl who said to a great rabbi that she wanted to sacrifice her life for Torah. Instead of an enthusiastic response, the rabbi said, 'Don't do us any favors.' So too, we should not feel like we are martyrs suffering for our children. After all, Judaism opposes human sacrifice."

ḤOL HAMOED (INTERMEDIATE DAYS OF SUKKOT)
Looking up to heaven

It seems that the more the world changes, the more revolutionary the idea of the sukka becomes. Building a sukka could well be seen as a subversive act for someone with an iPhone and an iPad. The beauty of this holiday lies in being outside and connecting with nature – finding the wooden boards, fixing them together for the walls of a makeshift hut, laying leafy branches over the top, and choosing the four species (lulav, etrog, myrtle, and willow). For many people (such as myself), the sukka is an annual encounter with the grass, the sun, the moon, the mosquitoes, and the ants. There is no app that can do the job for us. We ourselves have to take the hammer and nails, grasp the etrog, shake the four species, and once inside the sukka, raise our heads to check that there is just the right amount of shade and light coming through the branches of the roof.

Rabbi Nachman of Breslov passed away on the eighteenth of Tishrei, Ḥol HaMoed Sukkot 5571 (1810). He called upon us not only to connect with nature, but also with what is above nature. One of Rabbi Nachman's famous questions to his students was, "Have you looked up at heaven today?" Two hundred years ago, he was already warning us not to run from the elevator to the office, from the parking lot to the mall, without lifting our heads for a moment to reflect on a reality that exists above the material world. The festival of Sukkot is one week in the year in which we have no choice. We stop looking down at a screen and look up instead – at the leafy green branches and the heavens above.

A season for everything

Shabbat Ḥol HaMoed is here, and with it come the wisdom-filled words of King Solomon, including the book of Ecclesiastes, which we are accustomed to reading on Ḥol HaMoed Sukkot. It's one of the five *megillot* (scrolls or short books) that belong to the Writings section of the Hebrew Bible, and it includes King Solomon's famous words, "Everything has an appointed season, and there is a time for every matter under heaven. A time to give birth and a time to die; a time to plant and a time to uproot that which is planted. A time to kill and a time to heal; a time to break and a time to build. A time to weep and a time to laugh; a time of mourning and a time of dancing. A time to cast stones and a time to gather stones; a time to embrace and a time to refrain from embracing."

There are many commentaries on these words, but let us look at the simplest explanation: There is a time and a place for everything. In this frantic, confounding, global world of ours, there is a tendency to rush in and do everything simultaneously, erasing definitions and boundaries and mixing everything together. King Solomon reminds us of a basic truth: Everything has its own proper time and place. We go through different periods in life; it is full of change. There is both good and bad in our world. It is important to be aware and see what is needed at that time. Rabbi Avraham ibn Ezra wrote that "every person is obligated to do everything at its proper time." In order for each area to grow and blossom, it is important to make distinctions and separate different elements in our lives. And now Shabbat is coming, reminding us that there is a time for ordinary, workday matters, and a time for holiness. *Shabbat shalom.*

A sukka life

Each night of Sukkot, we traditionally invite one of the seven *Ushpizin* (visitors) into the sukka: Abraham, Isaac, Jacob, Joseph, Moses, Aaron, and David. What can we learn from this custom?

When we look at the story of their lives, we see that these seven figures had to continually confront challenges and crises. Abraham was called upon to leave his homeland and journey to the unknown Land of Israel, and from there to Egypt and back again. Isaac encountered enemies throughout his travels in the Land of Israel. Jacob was forced to flee to Haran, returned to the Land of Israel, and subsequently journeyed down to Egypt. Joseph was sold by his brothers and wound up in an Egyptian prison. Moses was hidden in a basket in the Nile River, grew up in Pharaoh's house, fled to Midian, and eventually returned to Egypt. His brother, Aaron, wandered with him for forty challenging years in the desert. David's life, too, was filled with war and rebellions.

Our forefathers lived transient "sukka lives" without permanent homes. But despite all their challenges, they continued to flourish. They learned, they educated, they brought good to the world, and so they became significant figures, powerful and eternal. They did not put everything on hold until "after the crisis." Just the opposite. They understood that the time is now, that life is lived within the maelstrom. Instead of waiting for peace and tranquility in order to do great things, they knew how to focus on what was important even while the world around them shook and trembled.

As we leave the sukka, this is the message we should take with us. No more excuses – the time is now.

SIMḤAT TORAH

A love letter

As Ḥol HaMoed Sukkot comes to a close, we celebrate Simḥat Torah, literally, "Rejoicing in the Torah." It is customary to remove the Torah scrolls from the ark and dance in circles with them around the *bima*, the raised platform in the center of the synagogue. In addition, all those present are called up to the Torah, including children.

As a child, I was a bookworm, and a member of several libraries. I have many memories of librarians saying "shh" to anyone caught making even the smallest noise in the library. On Simḥat Torah, it is the opposite. We dance and sing and wave the Torah scrolls, which may even be taken out into the street, and nobody says "shh." The Torah is not a book just for reading; it is more than that.

Here is a beautiful story about the special status of the Torah. Professor Nechama Leibowitz, a renowned teacher of Tanakh and recipient of the Israel Prize, used to sit for hours studying the Torah portion of the week, surrounded by dozens of commentary books.

When her students looked at her in astonishment, she would tell them: "This is not just about learning something new. It is about understanding a love letter. When a woman receives a love letter, she reads it over and over again, learns it by heart, and also thinks, 'Why did he put a comma here and a period there? Why did he choose this word and not another?' That's how we must read the Torah. We must go beneath the surface to understand and appreciate every detail in the love letter that we have been given."

This story is especially appropriate for Simḥat Torah, when we finish the cycle of reading the Torah and begin again, carefully rereading this eternal love letter of ours.

Carrying the Torah with us

How do we return to our everyday routine? Tishrei is a busy, eventful month, with Rosh HaShana, the Fast of Gedalia, the Ten Days of *Teshuva* and *Seliḥot*, Yom Kippur, Sukkot – but now what?

We were given the formula for going forward on the last day of this unique period of time. Our Sages relate that after all the festivals, God says to the nation of Israel, "It's not easy for Me to part from you. Stay with Me just one more day." So here we are; we stayed. But this day too will soon be over, and what then? It is for this reason that the day is called Simḥat Torah. It is the day we receive an answer as to how to return to our daily routine and yet retain the high of Tishrei. The secret for doing this is in our connection to the Torah.

On the last day of the festivals, we complete the book of Deuteronomy and begin the book of Genesis without missing a beat. The Torah portion of the week will continue to accompany us throughout the year. At the end of the Tishrei festivals, we need not detach ourselves and disengage, but instead we can use the inspiration of these holidays to incorporate Torah learning into our routine. After all, learning has been in the DNA of our people since we first appeared on the world stage thousands of years ago. We are the people of the book. It is not only our children who are (finally!) returning to school. All of us are beginning to learn anew – from the beginning. Have a good Torah year.

AḤAREI HAḤAGIM (AFTER THE HOLIDAYS)
Starting at the beginning

This week, we start reading the book of Genesis as we begin, once again, the cycle of weekly Torah reading. How can we muster enthusiasm for this? Didn't we learn back in kindergarten that "in the beginning, God created the heaven and the earth?"

Rabbi Moshe Shapira suggests we adopt the following approach:

"The cyclical pattern of learning Torah, seemingly repetitive, does not return to the same starting point each year. The Jewish perspective on history, the cycle of the Jewish year, the life cycle, and Torah learning is completely different. We can compare it to the turn of a screw or the rotary motion of a drill, where each turn goes deeper than the previous one. A spiral is created. Every craftsman knows that it is precisely the rotary movement of a screw or a drill that allows progress when penetrating stone walls, for example, in a place where the attempt to break through with head-on contact by means of a hammer and nails has failed."

There is power in rotary movement that allows us to advance a little with each turn. This is true in relationships between people and this is true when it comes to learning. When we begin the Torah all over again, we advance a little more each year. We persist, pave the way, and precisely because of this persistence we are able to reach a little further and find something new. We are not beginning, we are continuing to begin.

May we all enjoy success in this endeavor.

The lights of Tishrei

We return to our routines after the holidays that brought us so much joy. How do we come back down from the wonderful days of Tishrei?

First of all, we must remember that routine is the essence of our lives. The past month was overflowing with special days and moments, but most of life is not the high of a *Ne'ila* prayer. The prophet Zechariah asked: "Who would scorn a day of small things?" (4:10). In other words, we should not underestimate the small moments. Life is largely a mix of gray, such as the period we are entering now, and these in-between times are no less important.

Secondly, tools should be prepared to hold the light of the holidays. There are those who are accustomed to making a new resolution during the holidays, however small, that they will adhere to from now on, so that their routine will be less mundane.

Third, we must remember that the lights of the Tishrei holidays have not disappeared. Even if we don't feel it, we received an enormous spiritual boost during the past month. All the mitzvot we observed and the customs we followed had an effect on us, and this treasure has become part of us. Even if, at the moment, it cannot be seen on the surface, it has been absorbed into our souls and will radiate its light throughout the year.

In the book *HaKetav VeHakabbala*, it is written: "All the precious learning acquired by our souls during the holidays and the invitation to holiness that we experienced remain with us and will stay with us even after the holidays are over. The spiritual enlightenment to which we became accustomed during the holidays will not leave us when the holidays are over."

Ḥeshvan

THIRD OF ḤESHVAN: ANNIVERSARY OF THE DEATH OF RABBI OVADIA YOSEF

Simply a matter of love

Rabbi Ovadia Yosef was the Chief Sephardic Rabbi of Israel (Rishon LeZion), President of the Council of Torah Sages, recipient of the Israel Prize, and an esteemed halakhic authority. He passed away in 5774 (2013). He was the spiritual leader of the Shas political party, which I covered as a journalist for many years. I stood outside his home on HaKablan Street in the Har Nof neighborhood of Jerusalem on numerous occasions and spoke to the camera on insignificant matters such as government coalition crises, who would head the Shas Party list, and all kinds of bold political statements and apologies.

On the anniversary of the death of Rabbi Ovadia Yosef, it is fitting to talk about more important subjects, such as heritage, tradition, education, rectification, and self-improvement. His life's work was to return the Sephardic community to its former glory, with a strong sense of identity that had, on occasion, been robbed or compromised.

On various occasions I was privileged to interview his daughters, who shared some memories of their father with me:

47

Rivka Chikotai: "One picture in particular stands out for me from my childhood. Abba is sitting and learning in his room, and we children are arguing in a whisper. We learned to argue quietly so that we wouldn't disturb Abba while he was learning Torah. Ours was not an affluent home, but it was a very welcoming, hospitable home – we had many visitors and gave help to every needy and downcast soul. There was only one thing to which Abba was devoted as much as Torah: the public. At a rough estimate, the number of people our father counseled over the years must have numbered in the hundreds of thousands.

Adina Bar-Shalom: "During the period when Holocaust survivors who had lost their families, and sometimes their sanity, were arriving in Israel, children would sometimes mock them in the street for their behavior and appearance. Abba told the children in the neighborhood, 'These are holy people. You have no idea what they went through over there. We need to respect them and make life as easy as possible for them.'"

Daughter-in-law Yehudit Yosef, who looked after him in his home: "We saw someone who worked diligently without interruption for ninety-three years. The biggest challenge for him when he was ill was his inability to study and write, as this meant everything to him. Sometimes at night we would tell him to go to sleep and so he went to his bedroom, but he had a small library there, and we saw that he would just continue to study there instead. It was simply a matter of love."

"Ovadia is dust and ashes"

Here are a few stories I have heard over the years about Rav Ovadia Yosef and his legacy.

As he took the stage to speak, thousands would stand to cheer and applaud, often singing and dancing in his honor for many minutes. His close aides related that as he strode to the podium to speak, he would whisper to himself, "Ovadia is dust and ashes; Ovadia is dust and ashes." It was a constant reminder not to be blinded by honor, praise, and fame.

I myself once saw him cry in front of a crowd of thousands. "A million Jewish children in Israel and throughout the world do not know how to say *Shema Yisrael*," he said tearfully. He was greatly distressed that this basic Jewish knowledge, this heritage, was not accessible to all. Rav Ovadia therefore dedicated his life not only to personal study, but to ensuring that what he learned was widely available to everyone. Indeed, he perceived this as the reason for his success in learning: "If I was privileged to learn something in the Torah, it is only because I worked hard for others to under-stand the Torah as well."

One of his sons related the following: "On the first night he spent in the hospital, we saw that he was very upset. We asked him what was wrong and he replied, 'I have no books.' We ran to bring him a few volumes of Talmud so that he would feel better."

Rav Ovadia's funeral was the largest public event in the history of modern Israel, attended by approximately half a mil-lion people. His daughter Rivka later explained the depth of this love: "He wept with childless women, cared for children who had difficulty learning, and gave strength and encouragement to the unemployed and those struggling day to day. And so the people returned the love he had given them for ninety-three years."

SEVENTH OF ḤESHVAN
Waiting for everyone

On the seventh of Ḥeshvan, we start adding these words to our prayers: "Grant dew and rain for blessing." On this day, the entire nation of Israel changes its prayers and begins to ask for rain. Why exactly was this date chosen? A touching explanation appears in the Mishna (Taanit 1:3). Prior to the holiday of Sukkot, everyone would make a pilgrimage to Jerusalem. At the conclusion of the Sukkot holiday on the twenty-second of Tishrei, the public would begin to disperse and return home. Our Sages determined that we should wait fifteen days before asking God for rain – sufficient time for the last of the pilgrims to return home safely, including those who lived as far as the northern border, by the Euphrates River in present-day Iraq.

What sensitivity! After all, this was a farming community that waited expectantly for rain. Yet despite this, even though most of the nation had already arrived home and wanted the winter to come as soon as possible, the prayer for rain would not begin as long as someone, even a single person, would suffer from being stuck in the rain on the way home. The entire nation would wait until the last Jew had arrived home.

On the Tunisian island of Djerba, the Jewish community was accustomed to not returning its Torah scrolls to the ark after circling the pulpit with them on Simḥat Torah. This tradition had symbolic significance. As long as the pilgrims had not yet returned home in ancient times, so too, the Torah scrolls, in parallel fashion, would not be returned to their home in the ark. Only when the seventh of Ḥeshvan arrived would the Torah scrolls be returned to the ark in a special ceremony called *kiaman al sefarim* (returning the scrolls). And so, Ḥeshvan was transformed in these communities from a month usually known for its lack of holidays to a month with a holiday. The seventh of Ḥeshvan became a day for liturgical poetry and sermons, music and singing, and dancing and feasting in honor of the pilgrims and the Torah scrolls that had returned home.

Rain for the whole world

It is at this time of year that we read the story of Noah in the weekly Torah portion. Many commentators ask why we say "Avraham

Avinu" (our father Abraham) and not "Noaḥ Avinu" (our father Noah). After all, Abraham was descended from Noah, who is also described as a *tzaddik*, so why was he not chosen to be the father of the nation? Their answer is that Noah was passive with regard to the terrifying message he received in advance of the flood. He did not try to change the decree. He entered the ark he built in order to save himself, but he did not pray for others to be saved.

The Sephardic version of the prayer for rain reads as follows: "Grant dew and rain for a blessing over the entire face of the earth. Saturate the entire universe and satiate the entire world with Your goodness." This is not a prayer solely for the Land of Israel and for Jews, but for every land and every people. Even if we have relative quiet and material abundance, we care about the plight of the world and all of humanity. From the seventh of Ḥeshvan, we ask that everyone on earth be blessed with rain, abundance, and goodness.

Eyes toward heaven

If you live in a dry climate like ours and visit Europe, you cannot help but envy the unlimited supply of water there. In our country, the mood of an entire nation rises and falls as the water level in the Kinneret (Sea of Galilee) rises and falls. Strangely enough, the Torah singles out the Land of Israel for praise precisely for this reason. As opposed to Egypt, where the ever deep and flowing Nile River imparts a feeling of security, the Land of Israel is a land that "drinks water from heaven's rain."

In the arid Land of Israel, we constantly lift our eyes to heaven, hoping and praying for rain, thankful to God when it comes. There are many halakhot when it comes to prayers for rain, and the wording changes according to the season. God seems to be telling us: I am bringing you to a land in which you will be in touch with Me all the time. The Torah emphasizes: It is not the material wealth of our land that is worthy of praise, but its capacity to bring us closer to God.

ELEVENTH OF ḤESHVAN: ANNIVERSARY OF THE DEATH OF OUR MATRIARCH RACHEL

Like only a few days

The Torah describes how Rachel arrives with her flock at a well, which is covered by a heavy rock. It would usually take the joint effort of a few shepherds to lift the rock together. But what happened when Jacob took just one look at Rachel? "And it came to pass, when Jacob saw Rachel...that Jacob drew near and rolled the stone off the mouth of the well" (Gen. 29:10). Suddenly, the massive rock becomes light. This intensely powerful encounter with Rachel seems to defy gravity itself.

Jacob subsequently works for seven years in order to win the right to marry Rachel, and this period is described in the following beautiful verse: "So Jacob worked for Rachel seven years, but they appeared to him like a few days because of his love for her" (Gen. 29:20). Once again, we learn that our state of mind can indeed influence our physical reality. Seven years can become a few days. If previously, gravity was all but eliminated, now even the dimension of time loses its meaning.

Challenges become much easier to face and overcome when we have a goal and a purpose, and someone to inspire us.

When the celebration is canceled

"At the height of the corona pandemic, I filmed a class at Rachel's Tomb," Rabbanit Yemima Mizrachi told me. "There I met a sweet bat mitzva girl, who had to settle for a modest celebration with her family at Rachel's Tomb instead of a big party. I said to her, 'Do you know where you are? You are next to the one whose wedding celebration was canceled. This was not what Rachel imagined her wedding day would be like. She looked forward to it, waited, only to be disappointed when it was canceled. At the last minute, her sister Leah married Jacob in her place.

"You, too, did not want your bat mitzva day to look like this. You wanted a large celebration. But it was precisely from the deep pain of loss that Rachel told herself, 'It's true, they took away my celebration, but I will not allow them to take away my desire to do good. I do not want to cause embarrassment for my sister Leah.' At the height of her disappointment, Rachel thought about her sister and helped her. This is the power of Rachel, a power that can light up the world.

"Since the beginning of the pandemic, celebrations and dreams have been canceled for all of us. Our situation is not simple. But when it is dark for us, we should try to make sure it is not dark for others, to strive instead to bring them light. This is the greatness of Rachel. It is precisely when our celebrations have been canceled, when we feel the weight of what we are missing, that the time is right for accessing the powerful light-giving capacity of Rachel."

TWENTY-NINTH OF ḤESHVAN: SIGD
A reminder

How much time has elapsed since Yom Kippur? Thanks to *olim* (immigrants) from Ethiopia, we have a reminder every year: Sigd is celebrated on the twenty-ninth of Ḥeshvan, fifty days after Yom Kippur. It is observed as a day of fasting, purification, and renewal. Time does not pass by unnoticed. For Ethiopian Jewry, this date has always been set aside for *ḥeshbon hanefesh* (soul-searching), but it can serve as an opportunity for all of us to pause and consider a self-evaluation of sorts. It is a reminder that fifty days have passed since the *Ne'ila* prayer at the close of Yom Kippur, and with it, the resolutions we made at the beginning of the year. This is a good time to check how we are keeping up with them. Are we headed in the right direction?

Growing up with the Temple

Michal Avera Samuel, executive director of Fidel, an association that helps Ethiopians adapt to life in Israel, tells the following story:

"Until I was nine years old, I lived in a world in which the Holy Temple still stood. Like my parents and my teachers, I grew up with the belief that following the destruction of the First Temple, the Second Temple was built and is still standing today on elevated ground in Jerusalem. We believed that the city was literally made of gold. I heard descriptions of the priests in the Holy Temple and fell asleep to stories about the holiness of Jerusalem. I prayed to be worthy enough to return to Jerusalem, the spiritual center of the world.

"Belief in the holiness of Jerusalem was the driving force behind our education in Ethiopia, for both children and adults. An absolute truth passed down from generation to generation instilled in us an obligation to be pure of heart and action, so that one day we would be worthy of standing in the Temple. The power of these ideals gave us the strength to endure an exhausting trek through the desert, known as Operation Moses. We dreamt of Jerusalem as we buried those who died along the way and surrendered our possessions to bandits. Despite hunger and thirst, my family and I continued on foot, secure in the knowledge that, after so many generations, we would soon merit to be standing at the gates of the Holy Temple, on a hill chosen by God.

"We finally reached the Land of Israel, but discovered two thousand years late that the Holy Temple had been destroyed. To this day I have never been able to fill the vacuum I felt at that moment. I remember my father seeing Jews driving on Shabbat in Jerusalem. I could hear his heart breaking.

"It was only when I was older that I understood that I had, in fact, been privileged to grow up with the belief that the Temple still stood. My character was formed with an ongoing desire to be worthy of holiness. My parents lived with this desire into their old age, with the dream of being pure enough for Jerusalem. And I, unlike all of you, after all the generations that have come and gone since the destruction of the Temple, was fortunate to grow up differently. I, and those who grew up like me, truly feel the pain of the destruction. We fully understand the magnitude of the Temple's loss and its effect on our daily lives."

Kislev

NINETEENTH OF KISLEV

When Hasidism was set free

The nineteenth of Kislev is known as "Rosh HaShana for Hasidism."
Followers of Chabad, and many others who want to share the joy
of the occasion, celebrate in the streets of Israel and throughout
the world. On this day, more than two hundred years ago, the
founder of Chabad Hasidism, Rabbi Shneur Zalman of Liadi (the
Alter Rebbe), was released from a Russian prison, and in effect, the
hasidic movement was set free too. From that moment, it was as
though divine permission had been granted to freely teach and
spread the hasidic message. The book of Tanya, authored by the
Alter Rebbe, became a fundamental Jewish text throughout the
world.

On the nineteenth of Kislev, the daily learning cycle of the
Tanya comes to a close and then immediately begins all over again.
The following thoughts are taken from its pages:

"A Jew has a second soul that is an actual part of God." We
have an animal soul and a godly soul, both whirling within us. But
the second soul is a portion of godliness that dwells inside us. Do
we keep in mind that within ourselves, as well as within others,
there is an actual part of God?

"The mind rules the heart." Modern culture convinces us to go with the flow, to do whatever feels good. However, the truth is that human beings have the ability to control their desires, exercise self-restraint, and govern their emotions. It may not be easy, but it is possible. The mind is stronger than the heart.

"A little bit of light dispels a lot of darkness." We do not need to occupy ourselves with darkness, evil, and the failures of ourselves and others. If we only add a little light, the darkness will disappear.

Three simple truths, each one a revelation.

A party for completing the book of Tanya

Just a little bit each day. One paragraph, and then another. If I miss a day, then I will catch up the next day, or the one after, and failing that, I'll catch up on Shabbat morning. One paragraph at a time. And suddenly, it's the nineteenth of Kislev, "Rosh HaShana of Hasidism," and I realize in disbelief that I have actually completed the entire book of Tanya. *Nu*, really, I finished the Tanya? Just please don't quiz me on it – I didn't always understand what I read. Sometimes it seemed that I didn't even understand the majority. But I did understand that there was something great here, that there are secrets in this life. I understood that within the body there is a soul, that a perpetual struggle between good and evil takes place inside all of us, and we can and must prevail in this struggle at all times. Our thoughts, words, and actions are involved in this struggle and are all significant.

There is a reason the Tanya is called *Sefer HaBeinonim* (Book of the Intermediates). This refers to people who are neither completely saintly nor wholly wicked. They are the ones who are constantly struggling in the eternal battle between spiritual and material.

So no, I do not have great insight into Kabbala and the *Sefirot* (the Ten Attributes of God), but I understand that even if

I get upset with my children in the morning, or if I get stuck in a traffic jam and am going to be late, there is more going on. There is another dimension to life. There are other entire worlds beyond the physical world that we see, and every thought, word, and action of ours affects those worlds. Even as I covered elections, demonstrations, and court cases, the daily Tanya passage always shouted: There is something more, something beyond. There is an evil inclination and an inclination to do good, and the perpetual struggle between them. As we received news, to our dismay, about another terrorist attack, about the ongoing battle for our existence here, the daily Tanya passage reminded me: Don't forget the internal battle between our own good and evil sides, for this has an influence on the war between good and evil throughout the world. Of course, we need to deter and defeat the enemy outside, but the enemy within is equally important.

The Alter Rebbe set down his thoughts on all of this, on the "*dvash* and the *oketz*" (the honey and the sting), two hundred years ago in his book, the Tanya. Today, the nineteenth of Kislev, is the day he was released from prison. Whoever has walked side by side with him through this book during the past year now has the merit of finishing it, only to immediately begin the journey again and start reading from the beginning.

Soul music

What role does music play in our lives?

I was privileged to host one of the "Tzama" events, a women's evening of discussion and songs, in honor of the nineteenth of Kislev. I was in the company of singers Din-Din Aviv, Yuval Dayan, Ruchama Ben-Yosef, and Yafa Barkahn. From song to song, from *niggun* (hasidic tune) to *niggun*, it became clear to me that I have not understood and related to music properly.

During the evening, many "intentional *niggunim*" were sung. These are melodies composed by *tzaddikim* with a particular intention or subject in mind. Before each *niggun*, an explanation was given for the intention: This *niggun* can stimulate thoughts of *teshuva*; this *niggun* awakens gladness in the soul. It was a complete playlist of internal longings and service of Hashem.

Words for the songs came from King David, the Baal Shem Tov, and our daily prayer book. There is extraordinary depth and richness to our language, yet we miss so much of it as we superficially rush through the songs. Nevertheless, the *niggunim* that arouse the deepest feelings, as we learned in the course of the evening, are those without any words at all. They are beyond the limitation of words and pierce straight into the soul.

I learned that Rabbi Shalom Dovber Schneerson, the fifth Chabad Rebbe, once said, "A hasidic *niggun* strengthens hope, increases confidence, and radiates a joyfulness that glows in our homes and our families."

Music that is truly heard is not just an ornament or something playing in the background, it is an essential part of our character, of our very being. Yesterday I promised myself I would start to relate to music in a more significant way.

HANUKKA

What are the candles telling us?

The holiday of Hanukka marks the victory of the Hasmoneans in their rebellion against the Greeks, the rededication of the Holy Temple, and the miracle of the jug of oil. The Sages of Israel gave instructions to celebrate it by lighting candles, giving thanks, and rejoicing for eight days.

In the words of a famous hasidic saying: "We need to listen to what the candles are telling us." Here are several lessons our Sages learned from the *ḥanukkia* (Hanukka menora) that apply not only to Hanukka, but to our lives throughout the year.

1. **Appreciate the importance of tradition.** Unlike many other holidays, the events of Hanukka do not appear in the Tanakh, as they took place later. Instead, over many generations, the Sages developed the laws and customs we keep today. Thus, the essence of the holiday teaches us about the importance of tradition, the words of our Sages, and the Oral Torah.

2. **Prepare for darkness.** We do not light the candles in the morning, but rather when darkness falls. We are not taken aback by the darkness, but know that periods of darkness are part of life. It is precisely when darkness comes that we need to be prepared, knowing that such times call upon us to bring light.

3. **Illuminate the street.** We do not light candles solely to light up our homes on the inside, we also make sure our candles can be seen from the outside. We must strive to light up the street, the world outside.

4. **Increase light.** The manner of lighting on Hanukka is known as *"mosif veholekh"* (steadily adding or always doing more). Every day, another candle is added. It does not matter how much we did yesterday, we must move forward and do a little bit more each day.

5. **Strive for stability.** The candles are set in a certain place and must not be moved. A Jew must know that the light and values in his life are rooted in his soul, infuse his daily activities, and are secure. No one can confuse or move him from fulfilling his purpose.

6. **Give light to others so they can continue to shine.** After we light them, the candles continue to shine on their own. When we educate and influence others, we need to make

sure that what we teach is meaningful. If we do this, our students will give light on their own throughout their lives.

The Hanukka revolution

Rabbi Yerachmiel Yisrael Yitzchak Danziger was the head of the Alexander hasidic sect in Poland before perishing in the Holocaust together with most of his followers. Rabbi Danziger did not leave any children behind, but he did leave a remarkable book, "*Yismaḥ Yisrael.*" He describes the power and magnificence of lighting the Hanukka candles, as they connect us to the upper worlds. In anticipation of lighting the candles, pause for a moment and enjoy the following insight from his book:

"Even the simplest person, when lighting the holy menora, becomes a High Priest himself, and his home becomes a Holy Temple. He should contemplate prior to lighting that he is not just lighting oil lamps or wax candles, but that he is bringing up the light of the Six Days of Creation. Then he will approach this holy task with the fear and awe that accompanies the joy of doing a mitzva, and with the comprehension that a simple person like him has the privilege to bring about enormous revolutions in the upper worlds."

Who remembers Antiochus?

Rabbi Avigdor Nebenzahl, the rabbi of the Old City, wonders if anyone thinks about Antiochus today. Are there those who continue in his path and preserve his legacy? Is there an Antiochus Heritage Center? The question of whom we remember, and why, is pertinent in regard to Jacob and Esau, the brothers we are currently reading about in the book of Genesis. Jacob represents eternity, values, and long-term investment. Esau represents the here and now, violence, and wickedness. Rabbi Nebenzahl makes the following observation:

"Does anyone remember Jacob, dweller of tents? Of course we do. We mention him three times a day in the *Amida* prayer when we say 'the God of Jacob.' We are living the life and the legacy of our forefather Jacob. But does anyone remember Esau the hunter? Yes, whoever learns the Torah of Jacob...because outside the Torah there is no mention of Esau anywhere, as there is no mention of the other once-famous evil people of the past. And if it was not for the eternal nation of Jacob that mentions them, they would not be remembered at all. Where does Sennacherib the Great (the Assyrian king who laid siege to Jerusalem at the time of the First Temple) appear in our daily lives, and who today remembers Antiochus or Pharaoh?

"Regimes that seem strong and threatening become, in the end, footnotes in the history of the survivors who, now and then, remember the victories over their seemingly more powerful foes. As for evil, neither villains nor their unjust regimes prevail. Indeed, they ultimately cease to even exist."

A great light

"Shalom Sivan, my name is Alina," began a message I received on Hanukka during the pandemic. "I have been a Jew for one month. We hear a lot about the plight of business owners due to the pandemic, the challenges for singers and entertainers, and the distress of students. But it seems to me that no one speaks about the distress of those converting to Judaism at this time. We have had to endure the cancellation of Torah classes, we were only able to pray together on Zoom, and we had to celebrate holidays in lockdown that we so wanted to observe in the traditional way – through participation in large public prayer services.

"Due to lockdowns and isolation, time after time, I was unable to visit the wonderful host family that has accompanied me throughout this process. Yet these difficulties only strengthened my resolve, and I felt a greater sense of dedication and desire to overcome every obstacle in my path. I saw that the pandemic could change the world, but not my decision. I pushed myself and invested every effort so that I could finally stand before the *beit din* (rabbinical court) and join the Jewish nation.

"I am now fulfilling the mitzva of lighting Hanukka candles for the first time as a real Jew, and this is enormously symbolic for me. Judaism has brought tremendous light into my life. It is a light that penetrates all my thoughts. I learned that there is a deeper reality and my vision is no longer confined to superficial impressions. In the past, as an Israeli, I saw Hanukka as folklore, a nice legend that included eating doughnuts and *latkes* (potato pancakes) but not much more. Yet now these days are illuminated in their deepest meaning, as an expression of Jewish spirit, heroism, and immortality. Our Sages tell us that we should take the light of Hanukka and have it accompany us throughout the year. Hanukka teaches us to look at everything in life and illuminate it such that we see its true depth and vibrance. Happy Hanukka."

Thank you so much, Alina, and welcome.

Rabbi Shteinman's Hanukka

Rabbi Aharon Yehuda Leib Shteinman, a leader in the *ḥaredi* (ultra-Orthodox) community, passed away on the eve of Hanukka in 5778 (2017) at the age of 103. Here are some ideas about Hanukka that he shared with his students over the years:

"If we truly want to learn something from Hanukka, there is much to learn. Generally, people do not contemplate the essence of the holiday because they are too busy. They sing a little, eat something special – but we need to look at what the holiday teaches us: the power of individuals, the power of faith."

"Hanukka is a holiday about *pirsum hanes* (publicizing the miracle). When we are happy, naturally we want to share our happiness with others. At our wedding, we ourselves are a source of joy and we invite guests to share it with us. So too on Hanukka, we want to publicize the miracle and share it with others."

"Sometimes we fulfill a mitzva and feel nothing. There is no vitality. But Hanukka is a holiday of thanksgiving. We speak about the miracles in detail and express our gratitude for everything that happened, and in doing so we learn to pay attention to all the small details in our lives, appreciating every kindness and making sure that nothing good goes unnoticed or unfelt."

We are heroes too

A survey found that around 75 percent of Israelis light candles on each of the eight nights of Hanukka. This is an amazing statistic when you consider that no Antiochus is persecuting us and preventing us from living as Jews. There are many stories of our ancestors throughout the generations who hid, or were caught and tortured, during Hanukka. These stories are moving and important – but what about us? Our challenge is to preserve the fire and the fighting spirit of the Maccabees when no persecutor is chasing us and when the surrounding culture broadcasts the following message: "Bro, do whatever you like, it doesn't matter." How do we sustain our passion to fight for what is right when nothing is forbidden and everything is permitted? It is easier to maintain your identity when you are in a distinct war of good versus evil. But in today's open, permissive world, the line between right and wrong, between good and evil, has blurred. The challenge to acquire a strong sense of identity with purpose and meaning becomes critical.

Today, when we hear of fanaticism in the news, we may think of ideologies that sanctify death. But how do we sanctify life? How can Judaism ignite a positive fire, a fire that emits goodness, kindness, and light? Every year, during Hanukka, we are reminded that the vast majority of us are still interested in continuing the story of this holiday, from one generation to the next. There is a strong desire to preserve the values of our forefathers, the Hasmoneans, even in a world in which there is no Antiochus, no decrees from which to hide, and no enemy to rebel against. We maintain our ancient values out of joy, desire, and love. These days, this too is a type of heroism.

To simply look

What is the most difficult thing to do? To do nothing. On Hanukka, it is customary for women not to do any work for half an hour after the candles are lit, and to just sit and watch the flames. It is a time to think, to sing, to talk, to pray, simply to be there. Not to fry *sufganiyot* (doughnuts) in oil, not to answer messages, but just to sit next to the Hanukka lights.

"What do we lack most in the world today?" asks Rabbanit Yemima Mizrachi. "Self-composure, tranquility. You are about to send a text message to someone and then forget why and to whom you are sending it. You walk decisively into the kitchen and then stop to wonder, 'Why did I come in here?' During this half-hour after lighting the *ḥanukkia*, sit down and look at what you have. Stop trying so hard, stop running around and thinking that the light is to be found elsewhere. Just look at the flames and you will gain completely new insights. *'Lirotam bilvad'* – look only at them. That's all you need to do. Don't ruin these precious moments doing anything else."

Lighting on the second night of Hanukka, in jail

The LeZion Berina Institute in Beitar Illit is a high school for new immigrants from the former Soviet Union. Several years ago, Knesset member Yuli Edelstein visited there and told the students one of the most inspiring stories about Hanukka that I have ever heard.

Edelstein spoke about what happened on December 19, 1984, the day on which he was sentenced to three years in a forced labor camp in southern Siberia. The official charge was drug possession, but the real reason for his sentence was his Zionist and Jewish activism. Edelstein told his story as follows:

"This was after three months of solitary confinement. I arrived at the courthouse for the reading of my sentence. The courtroom was full of police and security officers. At a typical trial, it is permitted for relatives to come, but they filled every seat with security personnel in order to prevent family members from being seated. Only my wife and mother managed to get inside."

After the verdict was read, police surrounded twenty-six-year-old Edelstein and escorted him to his prison cell. On the way, he somehow managed to push his head through the ring of guards. He had only one thing to say to his wife, whom he had not seen in three months and might not see again for many years. What was it that he was compelled to shout at this moment? "Tanya, which candle is it today?"

The Russian security officers thought that the prisoner, upon hearing his heavy punishment, had gone mad. At first, his wife actually thought the same. She did not understand what he was talking about. But then he shouted again, "Tanya, which candle is it today?" Only after the third time did she come to her senses and shout back, "Tonight we light the second candle!" This was the morning of the first day of Hanukka 5744 (1984). Yuli Edelstein did not have a calendar in solitary confinement, but while listening to the verdict, he heard the secular date announced and realized that Hanukka was supposed to begin around that time of the year. It was important to him to know how many candles were to be lit that day.

Edelstein grew up in an assimilated family but had discovered Judaism and become observant. That evening, no longer in solitary confinement but in a cell with other prisoners, he somehow managed to get hold of two matches. He stood next to the bars of his jail cell window and lit the two matches.

"And so," he told the young students in Beitar Illit, "I stood at the window for several seconds until the matches burned my fingers. This was probably the shortest candle lighting in history, and I do not know if the mitzva even counted. But for me, on that night, a little bit of light dispelled an enormous darkness."

Respect yourself

If you do not respect yourself, no one will respect you either. This principle holds true not only in relationships and educating children (if you make yourself a doormat, you will not be respected by your spouse or children), but also as a nation. Living in Germany in the nineteenth century, Rabbi Samson Raphael Hirsch had to contend with many Jews who abandoned and belittled their traditions and culture. He wrote an article about Hanukka in which he reminded them that forsaking their culture would not help them integrate into German society. Here is a short and meaningful excerpt from that article, which is still pertinent to our situation today:

"To the extent that you respect your past and the holy figures from your history, the nations of the world will respect you. If you do not have a strong sense of your true identity, you may gain some measure of sympathy from the nations, but they will find it difficult to respect you. After all, if you belittle your past and do not honor your ancestors' graves and do not respect your Holy Temple and do not try to acquire proper knowledge of your Torah – how can you expect strangers to respect you and your heritage? Many delights will come to you at the price of denying the Torah, but do not anticipate respect. How great is the error of so-called progressive people, enlightened intellectuals, priests of the new. Go out and see what the Hanukka lights are telling you!"

Aharon Razel and the broken ḥanukkia

In his book *Life as a Melody,* songwriter and composer Aharon Razel retells the story of a certain *ḥanukkia* and a certain woman that touched him deeply:

"Grandma Miriam, a Holocaust survivor and family friend, is a permanent guest at our Hanukka candle lighting in the Nachlaot neighborhood of Jerusalem. When she leaves us, I accompany her a short distance to the open market of Mahane Yehuda. I once asked her if they were able to light candles in the concentration camps and she replied, 'In the transit camp in Holland, where we were first sent, we still had everything – *ḥanukkiot,* prayer books. But from there I was sent, as you know, to Bergen-Belsen, and there, of course, we had nothing.'

"We became silent, and I saw that she wanted to change the subject. I asked which *ḥanukkiot* they had lit in her childhood, and she answered: 'I will tell you something interesting. Once, I visited a museum with my daughter to see an exhibition of Jewish artifacts from Europe. We entered a room with *ḥanukkiot* from every country, and all of a sudden I saw a *ḥanukkia* exactly like the one we had in Holland. It was stolen by the Germans. They took us out of our home and then looted all our possessions. I continued looking and confirmed from several distinctive features that I recognized that it was definitely ours. I realized that, after many years, I was standing in front of our family's *ḥanukkia.* The curator of the exhibit told me that they had acquired it in Germany from a collection of wartime plunder.'

"I was deeply moved," Razel writes. "Seventy years ago, they sent a young woman on a train to her death, and they loaded her precious possessions onto a train going in a different direction. The Creator of the universe turns the world in mysterious ways, and He brought the same woman together with her *ḥanukkia* again, here in the Land of Israel! I began thinking about all the foreign cultures and empires, all the tanks and trains, the decrees and the wars that did everything to separate one girl from her *ḥanukkia* – to separate a Jew from her faith and her inner light – and they could not do it.

"Before parting from Grandma Miriam, I became curious and asked her, 'How were you certain that this was your *ḥanukkia*?' She was silent for a moment and said, 'A corner on the left side was broken in a very distinctive way, exactly as ours was at home. I remember my mother would say every year, 'We really need to fix this.'

"There is nothing more whole than a broken *ḥanukkia*, and there is nothing more beautiful than the hidden light that breaks forth from it."

(This is similar to the hasidic saying that there is nothing more whole than a broken heart.)

Lighting up the world from your window

"My ancestors were imprisoned in the ghetto in Frankfurt, Germany, for hundreds of years, where the gates were locked every evening," wrote Rabbi Chaim Navon in the *Makor Rishon* newspaper. Once, a German asked one of the ghetto elders, 'Isn't it humiliating to be locked up every night in the ghetto?' The wise old man answered him, 'It's not that we are locked in, but rather that you are locked out.'"

During the days of the corona pandemic, much of our outside activity has been limited or canceled. We have a choice in how to view this situation: Are we locked up on the inside, or is the world locked out? When our doors to the world are locked, perhaps it will remind us that home is, in the end, our most treasured place.

In the 1970s, Arik Einstein sang "You and I Will Change the World," the song reaching legendary status in Israel. Before we change the world, however, perhaps we need to fix ourselves and our immediate environs. Einstein's song "I Love Being at Home" may convey a more relevant message right now. Improvement begins on the inside and moves outward: First I will endeavor to change myself and those in my home, then I will improve my surroundings, and only then will I be able to better the world as a whole. That is the final stage of improvement, not the starting point.

Hanukka reminds us to begin inside the home. Our light will flood the streets of the city, but it will pour from within our homes. Those who want to transform the world build barricades in the streets. Those who want to illuminate the world light a candle at the entrance to their homes.

ZOT ḤANUKKA (THIS IS HANUKKA)
Gemar ḥatima tova (May you be sealed for a good judgment in the Book of Life)

Yes, that's the customary greeting at the close of Yom Kippur, but don't be confused.

Tonight we light eight candles, and until sunset tomorrow, it is still Hanukka. The eighth day of Hanukka, referred to as *"Zot Ḥanukka,"* is traditionally considered to be a significant day for prayer. Rebbe Yisrael Rozhin shared the following thoughts on this subject:

"The same positive responses that the righteous of the generation can bring about through their *Ne'ila* prayer on Yom Kippur can be brought about by any Jew with a simple prayer in front of the candles on the eighth night of Hanukka."

Some see this special day as the last day of the High Holy Days, and thus have the custom of repeating the greeting *"gemar ḥatima tova."* The journey toward *teshuva* that began on the first of Elul and continued through all the holidays of Tishrei ends now, on the last day of Hanukka, the day we are finally sealed in the Book of Life.

The ninth candle

That's it. The children have returned to school. The *ḥanukkia* has returned to the closet. We have gone from eight candles to none. Whereas on Hanukka we paused our daily routine in order to add more light to the world, we now find ourselves at work, in a traffic jam, or getting the children ready for bed.

In his classes that were held during Hanukka, Rabbi Shimshon David Pincus spoke about the ninth candle, the tenth candle, and all the days on which we do not light candles. He observed that we need to take the light of Hanukka with us going forward since the ninth day is also a miracle, and so is every other day. Our very routine is something extraordinary. On Hanukka, we learned to look at the world differently, to bring the holy into everyday life, to be thankful for what we have, and to see the goodness in a typical day and in the beauty of Creation. We celebrate the miracles "in those days," but also "at this time."

From Hanukka we learn that it is possible to look at the sun rising, or a child waking up in the morning, with the same wonder as the miracle of the little jug of oil. In doing so, we are able to bring what we learned during the past eight days of Hanukka into our winter routine and the reality of daily life.

May the light of Hanukka continue to shine for us throughout the year.

Tevet

What took place on this day?

Five important facts to know about the Tenth of Tevet:

1. The siege of the walls of Jerusalem began on this day in the year 588 BCE. Our ancestors awakened one morning to find that Nebuchadnezzar, the Babylonian king, had surrounded the walls of the city with his army. It is astounding that we remember and commemorate this event to this day, more than 2,500 years later.

2. The people of Jerusalem believed that the Holy Temple would never be destroyed, that their sovereignty here was eternal. The prophet Jeremiah tried to persuade them to live moral lives and adhere to the code of behavior prescribed for those dwelling in the Land of Israel, but they did not heed his words. The fast is a reminder that our existence here is dependent upon our behavior.

3. But wait a minute. The walls of Jerusalem were not breached on this day. The Holy Temple still stood. Destruction came

more than a year and a half later, on Tisha B'Av, so why do we fast today?

The fast marks the day that the siege of Jerusalem began, when the first sign of an approaching catastrophe was visible. At this point there was still time to change course and repair what needed to be fixed. The fast reminds us how important it is to notice the first cracks in our walls, to identify the beginnings of potential destruction – both on a national and personal level – and to nip impending disaster in the bud.

4. After the founding of the State, it was decided to mark today's date as *"Yom HaKaddish HaKlali"* (Day of *Kaddish*), in memory of those who perished in the Holocaust but whose date of death is unknown. Many survivors discovered that there was no record of when their relatives died, so they did not know when to say *Kaddish* for them, light a memorial candle, or learn Torah in their memories so as to assist in their souls' ascent in the upper worlds. If you have such relatives and do not know which day to mark their passing, the Tenth of Tevet is the day to remember them.

5. The Tenth of Tevet always arrives nearly one hundred days after Rosh HaShana; almost a third of the year has passed. This is an opportunity for soul-searching. It is a chance to reflect on where we were and where we are going, on the goals we set for ourselves on Rosh HaShana and where we are now, almost one hundred days later.

Understanding what we lost

"Really, does this seem logical? It makes sense to fast on the day the Holy Temple was destroyed, but on the day the siege of Jerusalem began? Isn't that an exaggeration?" a young boy asked of Rabbi Yoni Lavi. This is the answer he received:

"We have not exaggerated. There is only one Yom Kippur during the year, but there are no less than four different fasts for the Holy Temple. How can this be understood? It may not be possible to understand it. The loss of the Temple is unlike anything we know. The little we can understand is that we lost something so powerful and significant that no matter how much we weep, it will never be enough. And this is perhaps our greatest sorrow: We have no concept of our true loss. Indeed, this lack of understanding deserves a fast day of its own.

"For those who, despite this, desire to understand a little more, we can say this: The Holy Temple was not just any other large building made of stone, one among thousands that stood in Jerusalem. It was the beating heart of the nation of Israel, the channel that connected heaven and earth and made it possible for the Divine Presence to dwell in the Land of Israel. Ever since the Temple was lost, our world has been spiritually dormant. The body continues to exist, but the soul is missing. The side effects of this loss are all the physical and spiritual distress we have witnessed over the last two thousand years: from persecution and murder, suffering and disease, to materialism, depression, and confusion. The physical comfort and prosperity that surround us today are confusing and lead us astray. We see external displays of perfection, but what is most important, our inner spirituality, is lacking. Today is an opportunity to be reminded that the nation of Israel is like an exceptionally beautiful eagle born to soar up to heaven, but instead hops on the earth with broken wings and plucked feathers. Until we repair the damage and revive our spiritual pulse, we will not realize the enormous potential lying dormant within us as a nation."

The second generation

The Tenth of Tevet is now recognized as the day we recite a general *Kaddish* for all Holocaust victims whose date of death is unknown.

The following two stories were recently published about the second generation – the children of the survivors.

Yosef Rakover was a doctor for the partisans who fought in the Liptshan forests of Belarus during World War II. While in his hideout, he heard that Nazis had entered the area and were killing every Jew they found. Rather than be murdered, Yosef injected himself, as well as his wife and son, with heavy doses of morphine in order to pass out and appear dead. Tragically, his wife and son died of an overdose, while Yosef, rendered unconscious, was thrown onto a pile of corpses. The partisans found him, and not wanting to give up on their doctor, they miraculously resuscitated him. Yosef stayed with the partisan forces and continued to treat them. There he met Sonia, a nurse by profession who had also lost her spouse and son during the war. The couple survived, married, and made aliya (immigrated to Israel). One of their daughters is Professor Galia Rahav, head of the infectious disease unit at the Sheba Medical Center at Tel HaShomer. She participated in the torch lighting ceremony during Independence Day 5780 (2020) in honor of the medical teams fighting COVID-19.

The second story starts in Thessaloniki, Greece, where the Jewish community numbered approximately sixty thousand before World War II. More than fifty thousand of them were murdered by the Nazis. The Bourla family was among those who miraculously survived, and after the war a son, Avraham, was born. He grew up, earned a doctorate in biotechnology, and moved from Greece to the United States. Today, Avraham (Albert) Bourla is the CEO of Pfizer, the first drug company to develop a vaccine against COVID-19.

The children of Holocaust survivors and, by extension, all of us, have inherited a mission to save lives, to bring blessings to the world, to rehabilitate, to heal. It is something to consider on the day of the general *Kaddish* for Holocaust victims.

TWENTIETH OF TEVET:
ANNIVERSARY OF MAIMONIDES'S DEATH
From the writings of Maimonides

Maimonides, Rabbi Moshe Ben Maimon, known widely as the Rambam, was one of the greatest figures of our nation. He passed away on the twentieth of Tevet more than eight hundred years ago. It is difficult to truly capture the tremendous legacy that he left behind. He was a halakhic authority, philosopher, doctor, leader, and teacher. Some of his principles for living a Jewish life follow below:

"Anger is an exceedingly bad quality, and one should distance oneself from it to the extreme. Therefore, they [the Sages] instructed that one should distance oneself from anger so much that one accustoms himself not to feel [or react to] things which [would ordinarily] incite one to anger. And this is the ideal path."

"One who seeks perfection will criticize his own character traits consistently; he will examine his deeds and the qualities of his soul every day. And each time he sees himself going in an extreme direction, a healing correction will immediately be made."

"The joy that a person experiences in doing a mitzva – due to his love for God who commanded him to do it – is an extraordinarily great form of service."

"We must be especially careful to observe the mitzva of *tzedaka*, more so than any other positive mitzva, for *tzedaka* is a sign of the righteous lineage of our forefather Abraham. The throne of Israel is established and the religion of truth stands only on *tzedaka*. Israel will be redeemed through the merit of *tzedaka*."

"Whoever rebukes his friend should speak pleasantly with soft words, and tell him that he is only doing so for his own good, to bring him into the life of the World to Come."

"It is a foundation of faith in the Torah that if someone fulfills one of the 613 mitzvot in the proper manner, and does not do so for any ulterior motive but only out of love for the mitzva, he merits life in the World to Come."

"The Sages of blessed memory warned against calculating end times or when the Messiah would come because that would mislead and frustrate the masses when the predicted time arrived and he did not come."

"The purpose of learning Torah is to revere Heaven."

"It is fitting for one to contemplate the words of the holy Torah and to understand their meaning according to one's ability. If he cannot find a reason or understand its rationale, it does not mean it should be taken lightly, and it should not be dismissed as lacking in holiness."

"The prophets and sages did not desire the Messianic Era in order to rule the world, to come down on the nations or be exalted by them, or in order to eat, drink, and rejoice, but rather in order to be free to study the Torah and live by its wisdom."

Shevat

TU BISHVAT (FIFTEENTH OF SHEVAT)
An orange from the Land of Israel

Tu BiShvat, Rosh HaShana for the trees, first appears in the Mishna (Rosh HaShana 1:1) as the date on which the new year for fruit trees begins with regard to the many agricultural mitzvot that apply to the Land of Israel alone (tithing, first fruits, and others). For the Diaspora, Tu BiShvat has symbolized the longing for the Land of Israel. It is customary to eat the fruits that grow in Israel and to hold a Tu BiShvat Seder. In our generation, planting trees in the Land of Israel in honor of this day has become widely practiced.

Accountant Chaim Yoavi-Rabinovich was born in 5704 (1944) in Siberia, where his parents had been exiled. He was called Chaim because his parents had prayed that he would survive in an environment where the chances of a child enduring the freezing cold were slim. After the war, his family returned to Poland and made aliya in 5711 (1951). He described the Tu BiShvat of his childhood as follows:

"I was a six-year-old boy in the city of Lodz, Poland, in exile. The mood among the Jews of Poland, the remnant of a community of three million Jews, was uneasy. It appeared that the Soviet authorities had completely shut the gates for aliya to the Land of

Israel. In the Jewish schools they began to teach Polish, a clear sign that the Jews would remain there, apparently until the arrival of the Messiah.

"Just before Tu BiShvat, the Jewish community acquired a carton of oranges from the Land of Israel. They were not cheap and there was a limit of one orange per family.

"One snowy evening, my father, of blessed memory, returned from work and decided to take me, a six-year-old boy, to purchase the longed-for orange from the Land of Israel. My mother, of blessed memory, opposed her little boy going out on a snowy winter evening like this, but Father insisted. He took his tallit bag and we left together. We trudged through the snow and after finding the treasure we sought, Father gave me the responsibility of carrying the tallit bag, which contained the single orange that we bought.

"When we arrived home, we placed the orange in a large bowl in the center of our dining room table. Our Jewish neighbors came to see the orange from the Land of Israel. I also invited my friends to our home so that they too could see 'the orange from the Land of Israel.'

"On the night of Tu BiShvat, we sat around the table for a family feast. Father said the traditional blessing for fruit, '*Borei pri ha'etz*' (Creator of fruit from the tree) and '*sheheheyanu*' (Who has kept us alive – said when enjoying something new), took a knife, and cut the orange from the Land of Israel, then added this prayer which was customary to recite in the Diaspora on Tu BiShvat: 'May it be Your will, Hashem our God and God of our fathers, that You will bring us up to our land with joy, to eat from its fruit and to be satiated with its goodness.' I remember that my mother broke into bitter weeping as she was eating the orange. Our longings to leave the *galut* (exile) and make aliya to the Land of Israel were so strong.

"I kept the orange peels in a special cardboard box. The peels began to rot, but still I guarded them diligently. Several months later, with the help of a bribe, we received the long-awaited permit to finally leave Poland, where our family had lived for eight hundred years. I wanted to take the orange peels from Tu BiShvat with me, but my mother explained that in the Land of Israel we would have lots of oranges, so the peels remained behind in the impure land of Poland.

"If today I have a powerful love for the land of my forefathers and for its landscape, and if I have endangered my life for it on more than one occasion, the source and inspiration for this is most likely that single Tu BiShvat orange from the Land of Israel."

The wisdom of Tu BiShvat

A teacher once told me that there are four words which characterize the times in which we live: "I," "here," "now," and "everything." For this reason, Tu BiShvat is one of the most important days of the year: It is the antithesis of these four words. This festival of trees is celebrated not in spring but in winter – not when everything is already blooming and ripening, but at a time in which we do not yet see the results. We do not have everything right here and now, but instead we go out into nature and invest in the future. For now, we can only prepare the ground, plant, water, believe, and wait.

When our children were in kindergarten, one of their teachers planted seedlings next to the entrance and told the children, "Just wait a little while." This became one of their most meaningful lessons and perhaps even more so, one of ours, the busy parents who are always in a hurry. Each day, we would linger a little while by the plants at the entrance and learn from nature: how the plants were growing, what was blossoming, noticing the progress each day, little by little. It was a simple lesson about the value of patience, which cannot be taken for granted nowadays.

Ostensibly, it would appear that modern man is no longer bound to the slow processes of nature. He moves in an urban environment between house, parking lot, mall, elevator, car, and office, and in his hand he carries a device that controls him more than he controls it. But it is precisely because of this reality that Tu BiShvat forces us, once a year, to be reminded that there are slow and hidden processes, that there is development beneath the surface and we do not see everything the moment it happens, and therefore we must continue to cultivate a patience that only nature can teach.

This is true in almost every significant area of life: marriage, children's education, self-improvement and character refinement, and all areas of study. In an era in which we get nervous after five seconds if we do not see two blue check marks on our WhatsApp message, we are reminded once a year of the most important traits: restraint, perseverance, long-term investment, dedication, and devotion. It is these that, in the end, bring positive results and ripe fruits. Happy Tu BiShvat.

When there are no roots

The next story, which is fitting for Tu BiShvat and beyond, appears in the book *Eretz Agada* by Amos Bar.

"It was in the early days of Tel Aviv, the first Hebrew city. The city was tiny and the streets were still just deep tracts of sand, with no trees or gardens to be seen. One day, the residents of the small town of Tel Aviv heard the news that the minister of the British Colonies, Sir Winston Churchill, was coming to visit. The sitting mayor was Meir Dizengoff, after whom Dizengoff Street is named. The City Council convened to discuss how best to receive this important guest. At the end of a lengthy meeting, a decision was made to hold the reception on a street (today's Rothschild Boulevard) whose entire length would be planted with a colonnade of trees. However, the street was still bare, consisting only of piles of sand, with no trees. The members of the City Council considered what could be done and decided to plant temporary trees that would give the impression of a green and leafy boulevard. They found large trees outside the city and carefully uprooted them. The day before the visit, these were 'planted' in the sandy street through which the important minister would be passing. The residents of Tel Aviv lined the 'Avenue of Trees' in anticipation of greeting the guest of honor. As the crowd grew, they found themselves pushed up against the trees. Suddenly, the trees began to topple, one after another. Sir Winston Churchill, who was walking in the center of the boulevard, saw what was happening and laughed. Addressing Mayor Dizengoff, he remarked: 'You should know that nothing will last without roots.'"

FIRST SEMESTER REPORT CARDS
Half-time

It is the end of the first semester, and Israeli students are receiving their report cards. For the occasion, Rabbi Asher Cohen wrote the following to the girls studying at Orot Modi'in:

"What is the importance of the first semester report card? To me, it is like half-time at a basketball game. In the heat of the game and in constant motion, there is no time for necessary changes. There is no time to take a break and analyze the state of play. This is what half-time is for. During the break, the coach goes over the game plan with the players, citing which strengths have been demonstrated and where improvement is needed. And then they go out to play the second half. The report card gives us this interlude, an opportunity to stop and check ourselves.

"In the book of Ecclesiastes, King Solomon reveals a fundamental principle of life: 'A wise heart – on the right; a foolish heart – on the left.' There are many commentaries on this verse, but it can be understood as follows. When we read a Hebrew book, the pages we have already read are on the right side, and the pages on the left are yet to be read. On the right side we have proven ability, while on the left side lies undeveloped potential. The wise man looks first at what he has accomplished and only then at what he must fix going forward. King Solomon hints that we should not be too hard on ourselves, not emphasize our deficiencies, but rather focus on what we have achieved, on the knowledge we have accumulated, on the character traits that we merited to change and so forth. In the same way, we should look at the first semester report cards as a half-time break to assess what we have achieved and what we can work on, and then go out in the second half and be victorious."

Honest study

The following halakhic response reminds us that while many students focus on the grades when receiving their report cards, it is, in fact, the path leading to the grades that is more important.

Rabbi Chaim David Levi, recipient of the Israel Prize, served as the Sephardic Chief Rabbi of Tel Aviv and is the author of *Mekor Chaim*, a famous series of books on halakha. Among thousands of questions that he answered, he was once asked if it is permitted to copy from a friend's exam with the friend's permission. Here is his response:

"One of the six questions a person is asked after passing away is 'Did you negotiate in good faith?' (Shabbat 31a). The question relates to being honest and showing good faith in business transactions and by extension, in other areas of life as well. If a person must conduct himself in good faith where his livelihood is concerned, how much more so should this be the case in lesser matters. In addressing your question specifically, the issue is the prohibition of lying and cheating, even where we are not dealing with a take-home exam. A student who copies is lying to his teachers, and lying is such a serious prohibition that our Sages distanced themselves from anything even resembling a lie. When the question concerns copying from a friend's take-home exam, the student, as well as lying to his teachers, is damaging his character as he reneges on the trust that was placed in him. When someone allows his friend to copy from him, for whatever reason, he violates the prohibition against assisting another in committing a transgression. When a student cheats, he harms himself even further since his teachers do not know the true level of his knowledge. Therefore, take the straight and proper path chosen by King David, as the psalm says: 'Remove from me the way of falsehood'" (Ps. 119:29).

SHABBAT SHIRA (SABBATH OF SONG)

To sing or to complain

The Shabbat on which we read the *parasha* (Torah portion) of *Beshallaḥ* is called *Shabbat Shira*. It is named after the stirring song that the children of Israel sing in the *parasha* after the parting of the Red Sea: "Then Moses and the children of Israel sang this song to Hashem...." The accompanying *haftara* contains another song, the Song of Deborah.

An array of special practices has been adopted for this Shabbat in different communities. For example, some recite the song in the *parasha*, known as the "Song of the Sea," in a special melody, others stand while it is read, and some communities read the liturgical poem *"Yom Livsha"* by Yehuda HaLevi.

When we read the entire *parasha*, we discover something interesting. The Song of the Sea is followed by what one can call the "Song of Complaint." The children of Israel complain and long for the large pots of meat they had in Egypt. They even sigh, "If only we had died by the hand of Hashem" (Ex. 15:3).

In other words, a short time after an incredible miracle, after the people saw the Red Sea split and Pharaoh and his soldiers drown, they began to complain and show regret. It seems we are characterized by two desires – to sing and to complain. The question is: Which do we perpetuate? Which do we choose to remember, the song or the complaint? Which do we include in our prayer book? Ultimately, in our daily morning prayer, we repeat the Song of the Sea but not the complaint. On *Shabbat Shira*, we celebrate what is deserving of celebration: those moments when our forefathers saw reality in a proper and optimistic way, and began to sing.

Shabbat Shira with Avraham Fried

Avraham Fried, the great hasidic singer, once held a *tisch* (festive Friday night gathering) for *Shabbat Shira* in a Jerusalem hotel. An audience that was accustomed to seeing him on stage from afar now sat next to him and sang Shabbat songs together with him, without amplifiers or an orchestra. Fried explained to them the power of many voices singing together:

"What is a most confusing situation? When one person is speaking and then someone else starts to speak, and then another person starts to speak, and on and on. It is impossible to understand a single word. There is a well-known halakha (Torah law) that states, 'Two voices cannot be heard at once.' But where does each voice only add harmony and beauty? In music. And why is this so? Because here it is not the body speaking, but rather the soul. The world of music is higher than the world of speech. When our bodies speak, we do so as individuals. We are full of ourselves, full of materialistic and egoistic thoughts. But through singing together, the sound is more beautiful; it is full of power as our souls unite as one soul. This is the secret of song. So come, let us sing together."

Miriam's secret for successful teaching

In Hebrew, a tambourine is known as a "*tof Miriam*," literally "Miriam's drum." It never occurred to me that the *tof Miriam* so popular in kindergartens carries such an impressive legacy. It is, after all, named after Miriam the prophetess, sister of Moses. After the splitting of the Red Sea, Moses led the men in song and Miriam led the women. Rabbi Moshe Zvi Neriya learns an important principle from this. Moses and Aaron taught the men and Miriam taught the women, but there was a difference:

"Miriam was a more successful teacher than her brothers, Moses and Aaron," writes Rabbi Neriya. "The women of that generation were greater believers than the men. While the men led the sin of the Golden Calf, the sin of the spies, the sin of Korah, and others, the women were righteous. Who educated them so well, and how was it done? The secret of successful teaching lies in developing a personal connection with your students. When the Israelites rejoiced and sang the Song of the Sea, we are told that Miriam sang and danced together with the women. 'Miriam the prophetess, Aaron's sister, took a tambourine in her hand, and all the women came out after her with tambourines and with dances' (Ex. 15:16). This, surely, did not only happen when leaving Egypt, but must have repeated itself during the long years of wandering in the desert. Miriam was accustomed to joining the women in singing and dancing, creating lasting memories through shared experiences and a close connection with each of them."

Education, Rabbi Neriya explains, is achieved not only through lectures and classes but is based also on shared experiences, memories, melodies, and personal relationships. There is nothing like joining together in song to cultivate a rich education.

Adar

Increasing joy

"When Adar begins, we increase our joy" (Taanit 29a), and Adar begins today. But is it so easy to feel joy? Rebbe Nachman of Breslov explains that being joyful requires an investment. There is a common perception that a serious or melancholy person is probably a profound thinker, while the type of person who is always smiling and happy is most likely superficial. Yet Rebbe Nachman reveals to us that it is actually joy that brings us to profound and sensible thought, while sadness leads to reckless behavior and loss of control. He explains it as follows:

"Know that sadness makes it impossible to think sensibly, and therefore, in such a condition, it is difficult to find peace of mind. Only through joy can a person think sensibly and find peace of mind because joyfulness is freedom. Through joy, a person becomes free and is no longer shackled in exile."

In other words, sadness is a burden that prevents clarity of thought. Sadness and depression do not allow us to consider all options, make rational decisions, and provide guidance to others. When we are sad, we are no longer the driver at the wheel, and our mood takes us to undesirable places. At times like this, it is almost impossible for us to reason properly. Quality thinking requires an environment of optimism and tranquility, without any sadness. In other words, it is joy itself that makes it possible for us to take control of our lives and find the right path ahead.

The primrose path to sadness

The American Jewish sociologist Sol Herzig wrote a poignant article entitled "Six Simple Strategies for Achieving Misery" (see full article on Aish, www.aish.com). According to the author, these strategies are the surest ways to avoid happiness:

1. Cling to entitlement. You should always feel entitled. Life owes you something, and you were born to collect it. Always search for injustice in the fact that others have something that you don't have. Do not agree to any concession or compromise.

2. Everything is personal. Live under the assumption that everything happens with malicious intent, especially within your family. You just have to look for it. Jump at every opportunity to see events as final proof that you are not important to others.

3. Focus on your problems and think about them always. There is no point in having problems if you don't think about them constantly. Nurture within yourself the attitude that you cannot do anything until all your problems are solved.

4. Magnify everything. Why waste your time with a sense of proportion? Try to develop negative thinking in relation to every misstep and magnify it, removing any possibility for self-forgiveness.

5. Expect catastrophe. Always remember that dreadful, horrible things are bound to happen at any given moment. Allow your imagination to run wild – disease, destruction, terror attacks; the list is endless. Make sure you are not caught by surprise. Be alert.

6. Just say no thanks to gratitude. Relate to everything you have received in life as a given, without thanking those who brought about your success. Try to focus your thoughts on what you lack and not on what you have, paying attention to the disappointments in life and the bad that always accompanies the good.

After we adopt, or rather do not adopt, these six pieces of advice, let's all have a joyful month.

Do not give up on happiness

How do we become happy?

Rabbanit Yemima Mizrachi offers the following advice in her book *Invitation to Happiness*:

"We live in a happiness-challenged society. In many cases, happiness is simply a decision that we make, a choice. Women must choose to be happy. Instead of this, they may be giving up on happiness without even noticing they have done so, preoccupied as they are in the midst of everything else.

"These days, women expect themselves to do and achieve everything; to work, to educate, to be a success inside and outside the home, to host guests, to keep on steadily ticking, no matter what. Ours is a generation of perfectionism. And I say: Let go of some of what you do, just don't let go of happiness. Because what do you usually do? You stubbornly insist on doing everything, letting nothing go at all – except happiness.

"This is a mistake. A messy bed can be made. Marble can be polished. A work assignment can eventually be completed. But an unhappy woman? Oh, that is more serious than any of these things. So okay, you did not tell a bedtime story to the kids. You did not finish all the items on the list you were supposed to finish. You got frustrated again. But you neglected to write on your to-do list the task of smiling and having fun while doing so. Choose your tasks wisely; decide what to give up and what not to give up, but one thing you must not give up, heaven forbid, is your happiness today, right now."

SEVENTH OF ADAR:
ANNIVERSARY OF THE DEATH OF MOSES
Moses: The ultimate leader

Today is the seventh of Adar, the day of the passing of Moses. There is no grave over which we can pray, but thousands of years after his passing, this ultimate leader does not cease to influence us and shape our lives. Moses could have stayed in the palace of Pharaoh, but he went out to his suffering brothers. He was a stutterer and did not want any part of leadership, but proved that it is possible to lead a nation without charisma, but with the power of faith, prayer, and a higher purpose. He never stopped mediating between the people and God, and he dedicated himself to bringing them closer for forty years, until finally reaching the Promised Land, even though he never heard the words, "You have arrived." He revealed to us what an enormous privilege it is to enter the Land of Israel, but he himself did not gain this privilege. He did not put himself at the center, but elevated an ideal, a grand purpose and, in the end, promoted an ideology that is called by his name – *Torat Moshe* (the Torah of Moses).

On the anniversary of someone's passing, it is customary to study the books of the deceased so that his soul will ascend to ever higher places in heaven. Any Torah learning we do today comes from the Torah that Moses himself received on Mount Sinai, so whichever holy book we open, and whatever learning we do, it will all contribute to his soul's ascent.

In their memory

The seventh of Adar, the day of remembrance for Moses, whose burial place is unknown, has been declared a Memorial Day for all the casualties of Israel's wars whose burial place is also unknown.

An annual ceremony is held on Mount Herzl in Jerusalem to commemorate the memory of 566 soldiers. Among them are the twenty-three Palmach commandos who disappeared in a naval action during World War II, the forty-seven sailors killed when the battleship *Aḥi Eilat* was sunk in 1967, the sixty-nine-man crew of the Dakar submarine that sank in 1968, and others. On this day, we also mention the most recent casualties of war who have yet to be buried in Israel, Hadar Goldin and Oron Shaul, who were killed in Operation Protective Edge (the Gaza War of 2014).

The book *How to Build a Life: Studying Mesillat Yesharim with Hadar Goldin* includes commentary and thoughts that the young Hadar wrote to himself during his studies at the pre-military academy in Eli. Here is a reflection he wrote at the age of nineteen:

"Moses teaches me that the world within – containing all my values and aspirations, all my qualities and desires – is where I sustain myself and motivate myself to act. I learn from him to get up each morning and affirm that there is greatness in the world. This way of thinking builds character. To belong, to connect to greatness, to the kingship within me. Aspire to a grand belief, to a great life.... To what extent do you occupy yourself with little things, and how much do you direct your thoughts to something deeper? The function of Torah is to rejuvenate, refresh, and to return human thought to its proper, exalted place. I must occupy myself with Torah."

Let this be in memory of all the casualties of Israel's wars whose burial place is unknown.

SHABBAT ZAKHOR (SABBATH OF REMEMBRANCE)
What should we remember?

It is *Shabbat Zakhor*, the Shabbat before Purim. In addition to the weekly Torah portion that is read in synagogue, this Shabbat, a special portion of the Torah (Deut. 25:17–19) will also be read, beginning with the words: "Remember what Amalek did to you." Rabbi Yehuda Amital, head of Yeshivat Har Etzion, briefly explained the nature of the war we have today with Amalek. This is not war with a nation (has anyone seen an Amalekite on the street lately?), but with a worldview.

Rabbi Amital asks that we look carefully at the language used by the Torah in reference to Amalek: "that he happened upon you, on the way." The words "he happened upon you" represent randomness, "Amalekiteness," if you will. Our answer to this randomness is "on the way," to always be on the way to a specific destination.

"Amalek is an ideology that is, in essence, anti-ideology," writes Rabbi Amital. "Everything is permitted, everything is random, there is no absolute value to which we must cleave. Everything occurs by chance, haphazardly. It just happens.

"The nation of Israel, on the other hand, conducts itself differently. The first time Amalek attacked us, we were on the way from Egypt to the Land of Israel. The nation of Israel is always 'on the way.' It always has a direction, a purpose, and clear values to which it adheres. Every little detail in our lives is conducted while on this path. On *Shabbat Zakhor*, this is what we must remember."

The Amalekite ego

He's on top of the world, holds a most senior position, and yet, despite everything, he is not satisfied. The wicked Haman of the

Purim story is an Amalekite, a descendant of the nation that we read about on *Shabbat Zakhor*, the nation the Torah tells us to eliminate and whose memory we must erase. Amalek is characterized by several traits, one of which Haman clearly displays at the beginning of *Megillat Esther* (the Book of Esther). Haman is second in power to the king, highly influential, blessed with many children, and despite all this, he sighs: "And all this is worth nothing to me whenever I see Mordekhai the Jew sitting at the king's gate" (Est. 4:13). In other words, he may have oceans of honor but he feels the lack of even a single drop. Everyone bows down to him, but he needs Mordekhai to bow down too. If not, everything else is worthless.

The war against Amalek encompasses the war against traits such as this, focusing on the lack rather than the glass almost full. We need to fight our tendency toward self-obsession and pursuit of honor without gratitude or being joyful for what we have. When we make a noise to drown out Haman's name during the Megilla reading, it is also an attempt to erase his mindset.

TAANIT ESTHER (FAST OF ESTHER)
Women's Day in the Megilla

Taanit Esther is observed the day before Purim, a reminder of the fast that Queen Esther initiated before she approached her husband, King Ahasuerus, and asked him to rescind the decree to exterminate the Jews.

In contrast with the refined character of Esther, full of substance and strength, the Megilla describes another queen – Vashti. The Megilla opens with Ahasuerus hosting a lavish feast, flaunting his ornate vessels, fancy clothes, and other valuables. Among the precious ornaments and fine wines, he wants to show off one more possession: his wife, Vashti. The Megilla relates that he calls her in order "to show her beauty to the nations and the ministers, for she was indeed beautiful" (Est. 1:11).

This may sound incredibly primitive, but in fact, if we examine this honestly, we see that the mindset of Ahasuerus is still popular today. Whether in societies where women are treated like chattel, or in societies where advertisements, entertainment programs, and entire industries are based on external appearance alone, many people are still enslaved to the false ideal of superficial beauty.

Between the lines, the Megilla mocks Ahasuerus and demands a different attitude from its readers. This is something to think about on International Women's Day that happens to be marked at this time of year, and for that matter, on any other day.

Wearing royalty

A good friend shared a thought with me regarding what we can learn from *Taanit Esther*:

"Three powerful words describe how Esther prepared for her mission: 'Esther wore royalty' (Est. 5:1). Simply understood, this means she put on a crown and donned royal garments, but our Sages tell us that she wore the holy spirit of the Divine. She attached herself to the only royalty that matters, to the true King who runs the world, and not to Ahasuerus. Esther fasted and prayed, and all of the Jews fasted and prayed with her. Only then could she approach her mission with confidence that she was taking the correct course of action, without analyzing the pros and cons. She simply knew that this was her mission, a thought that gave her equanimity and removed all fears and doubts. To paraphrase a popular Israeli song, 'A woman suddenly wakes up one morning, feels she is a nation, and starts to go.' When Ahasuerus offers her 'even half the kingdom' (Est. 5:3), she does not ask for anything for herself; she asks only for her people. This is royalty.

These three words also infuse confidence within me during tense moments at home and at work: 'Esther wore royalty.' I try to 'wear royalty,' to truly feel that I know what I am doing, that this is my mission even if I should fail, and that I am part of a bigger, wide-reaching story."

PURIM

Under the costume

On the fourteenth of Adar, we celebrate Purim. The principal mitzvot of the holiday are reading *Megillat Esther*, giving gifts to the poor, sending packages of food and drink to friends, and holding a Purim feast. But the holiday includes many other customs too, such as those involving *raashanim* (noisemakers), eating *hamantaschen* (a type of cookie), and of course, dressing up in costumes. The Lubavitcher Rebbe called on us to learn an important lesson from the costumes:

"When we see someone dressed up on Purim as a frightening animal or a clown, it doesn't occur to us to be angry, or afraid, or to take that person seriously. After all, it's just a costume. But in everyday life, we frequently meet people who are seemingly 'dressed in costume.' This one is dressed up as arrogant, that one as vulgar, still another as apathetic and distant – but what we see is not a true reflection of who these people are. It is really just a costume.

"Sometimes our children also 'dress up' in a similar fashion and exhibit negative behaviors. In all these cases, we need to look deeper into what is inside, their purity and goodness, and reinforce it. We can even gently help them to remove the inauthentic costumes that they sometimes wear. We have seen many times how such a costume can suddenly come off and how, in a moment of truth, the true essence of the person underneath is revealed.

"The Jews of the Megilla disguised themselves as completely assimilated into the culture of ancient Persia, but when faced with Haman's decree to exterminate them, they were reminded of who they were and their true identity was suddenly revealed.

"We ourselves also wear a disguise sometimes. We need to look upon each other with love and understanding, knowing that whatever objectionable behavior we may see is not a reflection of the person within. We must take this awareness with us from Purim and keep it fresh in our minds throughout the year."

A revolutionary view of happiness

At the beginning of *Megillat Esther*, Ahasuerus holds an extravagant feast that is nothing more than an exercise in showing off. It is a celebration of silver, gold, and alcohol. In contrast to this mistaken and empty worldview of happiness, at the end of the Megilla, Esther brings the nation to a state of "light and happiness, joy and glory" (Est. 8:15). How does Esther express her joy? After the feast, she teaches us the meaning of true happiness through the mitzvot we perform until today:

First, happiness within the family circle – a festive meal that is an intimate family gathering and not just for show.

Second, happiness through community connections – sending packages of food and drink to one another to strengthen social ties.

And finally, helping those in need, caring for others and sending gifts to those who have less.

That is how we rejoice.

The equation of what makes us happy is flipped. Instead of conspicuous consumption and self-aggrandizement, we look outside of ourselves and learn that giving to those who surround us increases happiness. Instead of thinking that the more we receive, the happier we will be, Esther teaches us that the more we give, the happier we will be.

Writing our own Megilla

"*Megillat Esther* is a sequence of events that may be logically explained," Rabbi Adin Steinsaltz was accustomed to say. "The

Megilla does not include any supernatural miracle, but rather a series of events that, while surprising, are definitely possible. So what miracle do we celebrate on Purim? Why do we even need to read the Megilla?

"It appears that the incredible miracles and astonishing wonders celebrated on other holidays did not always have a long-term effect and did not always result in a dramatic change in the character of the people. *Megillat Esther*, however, presents us with a different perspective. Esther and Mordekhai are people of faith who pray and fast, and in the end succeed in saving the nation. There is nothing supernatural that occurs, but salvation still comes, hidden within gray reality, yet miraculous nevertheless. And it is precisely this that has left an indelible impression upon us for thousands of years."

Continuing this thought, Rabbi Steinsaltz calls on us to write "the Megilla of our own lives," to find the hidden within the revealed: "We must identify matters of this kind by opening our eyes and paying attention. If a person sits and takes stock on a daily and monthly basis, and considers the events in his life, connecting everything, however big or small, that happens, it will bring him to understand the meaning of our prayers: 'Your miracles are with us every day.' Therefore we say on Purim, 'Everything was turned upside down.' We need to radically change the way we look at gray reality and uncover the goodness that is concealed within it."

Breaking boundaries

Purim parties are often associated with mayhem, but an educator of at-risk youth shared the following idea with me:

"We may not realize it, but actually are all set in our ways. We make decisions regarding ourselves based on thinking, 'I'm like this and this and it's impossible to change.' But on Purim, everything is in flux and it's possible to change our state of mind. This is an opportunity for personal transformation since 'everything is reversed' and we can break through our barriers. Generally, when we speak about breaking barriers or crossing borders, the implication is negative. When someone speaks about having the courage to do things that are not done all year long, we assume some undesirable behavior is involved. But is there a second option? What about breaking through my barriers in order to do good things that I always wanted to do? What about seizing courage and daring to go in a more positive direction? Who said that excess on Purim must bring a person to a low and ugly place, rather than opening him up to a more spiritual and joyful place? At this time of year, we permit ourselves to let loose. Who says the intention cannot be to let loose in a new, elevated, and wonderful direction?"

The right choice

I heard the following explanation on the meaning of Purim from Ron Dermer. When he was Israel's Ambassador to the United States, he hosted a Purim party where he explained how he understood the Megilla, both historically and in our times.

"Faced with Haman's vile decree and the threat to exterminate all the Jews, Mordekhai comes to Esther and tells her something fascinating. Usually, we would expect Mordekhai to plead before Esther, to beg her to save the Jewish people. But here, he does not plead. Instead, he encourages her to make the right decision: 'Do not think that you will escape [the fate of] all the Jews by being in the king's palace. For if you remain silent at this time, relief and salvation will come to the Jews from another source, and you and the house of your father will be lost. And who knows if it is not for just such a moment that you reached this royal position' (Est. 4:13–14). Mordekhai does not ask Esther to save the Jewish people, but to save herself. The nation will survive, the question is what role Esther will play. Esther chose correctly, and therefore we sit here tonight and read *Megillat "Esther"* in her name. If she had chosen otherwise, we would still be here – 'relief and salvation will come to the Jews from another source' – but Esther would have made an eternal error.

"We too must check where our life's path is leading us and what our role will be, not only in saving others but in saving ourselves, in connecting with our destiny and with the eternal destiny of the Jewish people."

A guide to identifying true happiness

Rabbi Yoni Lavi offers a short guide to identifying genuine happiness:

"It is difficult to counterfeit money. Extensive measures have been taken to prevent criminals making a fortune in the manufacture of fake money. Happiness, on the other hand, can easily be faked. It is easy enough to plaster a smile on your face and laugh loudly, and to fool everyone (and even yourself) that you are the happiest person around. How does one distinguish between fake and genuine happiness? Here are some of the signs:

"Genuine happiness is not fueled by external conditions such as loud music or alcoholic drinks. Nor is it connected to how much money you earn or how many daily 'likes' you got today. Your happiness is delicate yet independent, felt on the outside yet emanating from within. It is not based on what you have, but largely on who you are.

"Fake happiness comes from distancing yourself and escaping from reality. It obligates you to 'go out' in order to 'really live,' to search for happiness in far-off regions as opposed to finding it close by – in family, work, and familiar surroundings.

"Genuine happiness does not wait for special days or events in order to appear. It is present on the ordinary, gray days of fall, and even on the gloomy, cold days of winter.

"Fake happiness is short-lived. Fake happiness does not usually last more than a few minutes, or at best, a few hours. Often, once it is gone, it leaves a bitter aftertaste, as if you ate something rotten.

"Fake happiness often comes at someone else's expense. It is the sister of cynicism, the cousin of callousness and superiority, and its family name is selfishness.

"True happiness, by contrast, does not include mocking another person, and is not limited to a closed, elitist group. In fact, it doubles when we share it with others. Happiness like this gives us strength and motivation to go forward, and its expiry date is not the next day.

"Genuine happiness is closely connected to faith and a positive outlook, contentment with one's lot in life, and with seeing the glass half full. It does not ignore the flaws and difficulties that exist in reality, but knows how to put them in proper perspective. True happiness knows how to be impressed and get excited from even the small, everyday things, and does not wait for a big 'boom' to awaken. It refuses to take for granted the infinite sea of gifts in which we swim, and remembers to say thank you every morning for everything there is.

"Whoever settles for a fake product misses the opportunity to experience the real thing – sincere happiness, deep and internal, one of the most wonderful things in the world. Beware of imitations."

Real poverty is lack of knowledge

Ostensibly, gifts for the needy define our duty to the poor on Purim. A little *tzedaka* and we've fulfilled our obligation. In the Gemara, however, our Sages state: "There is no poverty except in knowledge" (Nedarim 41a). In other words, poverty does not only relate to finance, it concerns wisdom and knowledge as well. In fact, there are people below the poverty line in these areas too.

Further to this, in his book *Sefat Emet*, a collection of thoughts and commentary by the Rebbe of Gur, Rabbi Yehuda

Aryeh Leib Alter, he explains that every one of us is actually both poor and rich. We all fall into the category of "poor in intelligence" since we do not know enough and can always learn from others. But equally, each person is considered rich since he can impart his own knowledge to someone who is in need of it.

The *Sefat Emet* describes "gifts for the needy" on Purim: "After their salvation, the people will gather together as a single unit. Those rich in Torah will give to the poor in Torah. And scholars will receive from one another. Because every scholar has something special to give, and each needs to receive something from the other, joining together as a single unit."

Torah and knowledge are also "gifts for the needy," and should be given and received throughout the year.

An American Purim

"Hello, my name is Adi Yarchi, an emissary of the World Zionist Organization in Connecticut. I wanted to send a message from afar. In Israel, everyone knows when Purim is approaching. It's everywhere: in toy stores, grocery stores, advertisements, on buses, and in the street. In Israel, you can feel Purim in the air as Judaism simply surrounds you. Here in America, this week marked Saint Patrick's Day, which is widely publicized. On this Christian holiday, everything is decorated with green clover. Shortly afterward, Easter arrives with Easter eggs and rabbits everywhere. Purim masks? Noisemakers? Perhaps if we make a special trip to Brooklyn, we will see some of them. If we do not make an effort to create a Purim atmosphere ourselves, we will feel nothing. That is why we strive to expose the next generation to their heritage, and to have them remain Jews out of love and choice. For many, the only opportunity to eat in a sukka, for example, is at school. At Hanukka time, we pass out chocolate coins and make a huge effort to bring the light of Hanukka into their lives, and with Purim approaching, we are also working hard. It's a challenge. So I wanted to remind you that even during these difficult days – both politically and from a security standpoint – what a privilege it is to live in the Land of Israel. Things that we can see from here are not always so clear from there. Have a happy Purim."

Remembering Shushan Purim

Most of the world celebrates Purim on the fourteenth of Adar, but in Jerusalem, which according to tradition was a walled city in the days of Joshua, Purim is celebrated the next day and is known as Shushan Purim.

Rabbi Abraham Isaac HaCohen Kook, who crafted an inspiring maxim to accompany each month of the year, wrote the following wonderful thought about the month of Adar: "Those who mention cities with walls from the days of Joshua cannot remain slaves of Ahasuerus." In other words, whoever always remembers a built-up Jerusalem, surrounded by walls from the days of Joshua, will not remain enslaved.

In the depths of exile, in the days of *Megillat Esther*, when the Land of Israel was desolate and in ruins, our Sages sought to remember the land, the days of Joshua, and the city of Jerusalem in its past glory, in the hope that Jerusalem would soon be built again.

Rabbi Kook states that those who remember their past will yet be privileged to enjoy a great and glorious future. One day, they will leave exile for freedom. An awareness so deep and ancient must ultimately lead to complete fulfillment of the dream. The nation will become a light unto the world and will never be enslaved again.

Happy Purim, Jerusalem.

Nisan

BLESSING THE FRUIT TREES
Don't miss out!

From the beginning of the month of Nisan until the end of the month, it is customary to bless budding fruit trees. Upon seeing two such trees, we say: "Blessed are You, Hashem our God, King of the universe, who has made nothing lacking in His world, and created in it goodly creatures and goodly trees to give human beings pleasure."

Rabbi Itamar Heiken went out with his students to bless the trees and returned with the following insight:

"We are bound to experience a loss of sensitivity and a diminished sense of excitement, not always seeing the beauty of nature and the enchantment of life. Our Sages say: 'The wicked during their lifetime are regarded as dead. For what reason? Upon seeing the sun rise, they do not bless 'the One who forms light,' and upon seeing the sun set, they do not bless 'the One who brings on evenings.' They eat and drink and do not bless. However, the righteous say a blessing on everything that they eat and drink and see and hear' (*Midrash Tanḥuma, Vezot Haberakha*).

Our Sages were concerned that we would live our lives without paying attention to the rising and the setting of the sun, without seeing all the good in the world, without being grateful for it. In the month of Nisan, just once a year, in the spring, we go outside and bless the trees. It is best not to postpone this mitzva, but to stop for a moment in the midst of work, study, or doing errands, and take a trip into nature, or even visit an urban landscape nearby, where two fruit trees are blossoming. Take a moment to look at them and to bless them. It is so simple and yet so beautiful. And then, should they ask you, 'What did you do today?' – as in the song by Aharon Razel – you will answer: 'Today I recited the blessing over the trees. Today, despite the frenzy of life, I remembered to take a moment and appreciate nature.'"

PREPARATIONS FOR PASSOVER
We are rich

The days of cleaning for Passover are not the easiest days of the year, to say the least. But Dr. Miri Kahana from Efrata Teachers College brings a different perspective for this time of year.

"I wanted to share a thought to which I continually return: All of this arduous cleaning is only because we are rich. Not just me, but all of us. We live with our families in our own homes. There is a separate room for the parents, a kitchen, a shower, and a bathroom. Our homes are full of furniture, clothes, appliances, and food. Our children have so much to eat that they have the luxury of forgetting unopened bags of snacks in their desk drawers and leave sandwiches that they did not even taste in their backpacks. Our lives are very far removed from those distant halakhic discussions regarding a public oven for several families; or the issue of a poor person's cloak, taken as collateral for a loan, that must be returned each night since the poor person sleeps in his cloak; or the matter of a poor person washing his only shirt on Erev Shabbat (Sabbath eve), despite the prohibition of laundering on this day (prior to the era of washing machines).

"Despite the difficulties and challenges of our generation, I am certain that all of us have at least one great-grandfather who would be overwhelmed with surprise and joy if he could see the prosperity in which his great-grandchildren live. Therefore, every once in a while, I remind myself to stop complaining about how much we still have to clean or cook, and simply focus instead on how much we have."

Clean and renew

To throw or not to throw, that is the question. Time and again at this time of year we find ourselves looking at dishes, books, clothes and wondering if their place is in the closet or in the trash. Many of these were in exactly the same place a year ago and we have not used them since. Rebbe Pinchas from Koritz, one of the founders of the hasidic movement, wrote the following in his book *Imrei Pinḥas*.

"The exerted efforts undertaken around the house before Passover allow a person to forget his troubles. It is as if he is shedding an old suit, an older version of himself, and donning a new one. Only through the pressure of cleaning for Passover can he receive new vitality and new light. Therefore, a person should throw away things for which he has no need; this is the essence of Passover cleaning."

In other words, cleaning and reorganizing give us energy and a new spark, and the reason for cleaning is to simply throw away what we don't need. The things we collect and do not use simply drain us of energy. They take up space in the home, but also within our souls. Every unnecessary object represents a false desire, a distraction. We need to clean out extraneous things in order to live a more focused life, to live with what we truly need. We should also leave space for new things, especially new blessings to enter our lives, if only we will let them.

They will not steal our Passover

The preparations for Passover are likely to confound us. So writes Aviad Hezni, an officer in the military rabbinate:

"Today at a bus stop I heard two older women saying that there is nothing to eat on Passover. Yesterday, a friend let slip the remark, in evident sadness, that matza upsets his stomach. During the last few days, I have encountered dozens of social media posts regarding the distress brought on by cleaning for the holiday. Friends, Passover has been stolen from us!

"Passover is the most revolutionary holiday in human history. A nation of slaves dared to provoke the greatest world power and were liberated, thanks to incredible miracles. Passover is the holiday that celebrates faith. Passover is about taking a bruised and broken slave and whispering in his ear that he is more than a number. He has dreams, feelings, and phenomenal strength within himself. And above all – he has a mission. Passover is for telling him about previous generations, teaching him about their true faith, and persuading him that he can follow in their footsteps.

"Passover celebrates the extraordinary struggle of a nation, its readiness to travel on a long journey. It commemorates a process of radical refinement. Passover is a holiday of simplicity: just flour, water, and an oven. It teaches us to find pleasure in simple things that lack sophistication. Think about Passover. Live Passover. We cannot allow a shallow conversation to steal the Passover spirit from us. In truth, our 'suffering' comes from decisions we make to embark on exaggerated cleaning projects. Passover halakhot are innocuous and simple and are intended to accompany a process of inner, spiritual striving. We cannot allow the secondary importance of cleaning or what we can't eat to become the primary focus. We cannot allow Passover to be stolen from us."

One more Passover recipe

The hectic days before Passover are bound to be filled with last-minute errands, waiting in line, stress, shouting, and conflict. Eight hundred years ago, on the eleventh of Nisan, Nahmanides, Rabbi Moshe Ben Nahman (also known as the Ramban), passed away. He was one of our nation's greatest thinkers and commentators. He left behind *Iggeret HaRamban*, an ethical will written for his son, which he recommends we read at least once a week. Here is some of the practical advice found within:

"Accustom yourself to speak all of your words calmly, to every person, all the time. In doing so you will prevent your anger from flaring, which is a bad attribute in a human being and may cause you to sin. And so our rabbis said, 'Anyone who gets angry – all of *Gehinnom* rules over him.'"

"When you are saved from anger, the quality of humility will enter your heart; that is the best of all good traits."

"Consider everyone as greater than yourself. If someone is wise or wealthy, you should give that person respect. If someone is poor and you are wealthier or wiser, consider yourself to be more at fault and less worthy than the other person, since when that person sins it is inadvertent, while you act knowingly."

Calm speech, humility, respect toward the other person no matter who they are, fleeing from anger – a wonderful recipe for the days before Passover.

SHABBAT HAGADOL (THE GREAT SABBATH)
What will redemption look like?

On the Shabbat before Passover, the *haftara* includes a description of the day of our final redemption, as depicted in the words of the prophet Malachi: "the great and awesome day of Hashem" (Mal. 3:23). Therefore this Shabbat is called "The Great Sabbath."

How does the prophet describe the end of days, in a text so central that we read it every year before Passover? He depicts wars and struggles, and then reaches the climactic event. As the days of the Messiah approach, Elijah the prophet will precede him in order to "turn the hearts of parents to their children, and the hearts of children to their parents."

Many commentators focus on this surprising prophecy that casts reconciliation between parents and children as the foundation for universal rectification, as if the end of family quarrels and tension between the generations is the key. Is a "supernanny" all we need in order to advance the cause of humanity? Is healthy communication between the generations and a genuine bond between adults and youth all that important?

Apparently, yes. It is not a coincidence that the Passover Seder is constructed around the family table. It is not enough for the adults to recount the story of the Exodus from Egypt. It is not enough for the children to learn about it in kindergarten. We have to connect the generations, connect our hearts, and in doing so we will strengthen each other. This unity is essential to the process of redemption.

THE FESTIVAL OF PASSOVER
What is freedom?

Passover is celebrated in the middle of the month of Nisan for seven days and includes many mitzvot: the obligation to eat matza, the prohibition on eating *hametz* (bread and other leavened products), telling the story of the Exodus from Egypt, drinking four cups of wine on Seder night, and many more.

In the festival prayers, Passover is named "the time of our freedom." Rabbi Eyal Vered from Petah Tikva and a rabbi at Machon Meir has attempted to translate the magnificent concept of freedom into everyday terms:

"Freedom is recognizing the little red button that shuts off our electronic devices, and using it now and again.

Freedom is taking only what we need from a lavish wedding buffet, where there is enough food for a herd of elephants and far too much for ordinary people.

Freedom is the capacity not to hear or read *lashon hara* (derogatory language), even though it bubbles up all around us.

Freedom is the ability to tell your employer that you have a spouse and children and therefore cannot work around the clock, that you cannot leave home so early in the morning that the children are still asleep and then return at night long after they are asleep again. You have other priorities in life in addition to work. And before you tell this to your employer, you need to tell this to yourself.

Freedom is knowing how to live within your means, not spending money you don't have (i.e., not being perpetually in overdraft).

Freedom is the capacity to remain silent, not to react to everything, to hold your tongue during an argument.

Freedom is striving to find the good where no one else sees it, and articulating it with passion. It is seeing reality in a positive light and not falling into the pit of complaint and discontent. It is being joyful and giving thanks, and knowing how to make things better.

Freedom is not honking in anger at the driver in front of us when the traffic light turns green, but rather signaling to him gently with our headlights.

Freedom is the ability to see each individual not as a means, as someone to exploit, but rather as a person in his or her own right.

Rabbi Yehuda Halevi wrote: "Slaves to time are abject slaves; only the slaves of Hashem are free." The Statue of Liberty has its place, yet freedom is not just a symbol, but the essence of who we are as Jews. It is the complete expression of our personality, both as individuals and as a nation. Happy festival of freedom.

The Mayflower and the Exodus

In 1947, David Ben-Gurion spoke before a United Nations investigative committee that had arrived in Israel. In order to explain our connection to the Land of Israel, he recounted the following Passover story:

"Three hundred years ago, a ship called the Mayflower set sail for the New World. This was a seminal event in the history of both England and America. But I want to know if there is a single Englishman who knows exactly what date the ship embarked. How many Americans know this? Do they know how many people were on board and what kind of bread they ate as they departed?

"Three thousand years before the Mayflower, the Jews left Egypt, and every Jew in the world, including those in America and the Soviet Union, knows that the date they left was the fifteenth of Nisan. And everyone knows exactly what kind of bread the Jews ate: matza. To this day, Jews throughout the world eat this same matza on the fifteenth of Nisan – in America, in Russia, and in a multitude of other countries. They tell the story of the painful experience of the Jews when they went into Egyptian exile and of their redemption when they finally left, and they finish the story with two inspiring declarations: 'This year we are slaves; next year we will be free,' and 'This year we are here; next year in Jerusalem – in Zion, in the Land of Israel.' These longings are the nature of every Jew."

Natan Sharansky and the challenge of freedom

I was once privileged to interview Natan Sharansky. He recalled a unique and historic Seder night in a Russian prison, where he did not have matza but spoke all night long of slavery and freedom to the other prisoners. But then Sharansky added something. It was a message not about living through the Holocaust or enduring a prison sentence behind the Iron Curtain, but about the challenge facing every one of us:

"Imagine someone in a Siberian prison and, by contrast, someone walking leisurely down the street in Israel. Which one of the two is free and which one is a slave? Amazingly, in prison it was easier for me to remain free. In that situation, it was clear who and what was good and who and what was bad, and it was easier to cling to the good. By contrast, it is precisely in an open society that a person faces waves of challenges and distractions, making it difficult to choose with a pure heart and authentic desire. The line between good and bad is blurred, powerful market forces are at work, and it is easier to succumb to temptation. A person feels that he is free and is not aware of his slavery. It is especially in this sort of society, in which we are privileged to live, that a person needs to work hard in order to be genuinely free."

Hadar Goldin's Passover message

In the course of a few years, Hadar Goldin has achieved legendary status. He was an IDF officer killed in Operation *Tzuk Eitan* (Protective Edge) in Gaza in 2014, and the struggle to bring him to Israel for burial is still ongoing. When Goldin was seventeen years old and a leader in the Bnei Akiva movement in Kfar Saba, he wrote a pre-Passover message about the choice to be a slave or a free man:

"Well, we have celebrated Purim and are now approaching Passover. What is special about Purim and Passover is that they are both full of stories. During these holidays, all of us become storytellers! On Purim, we tell the story of *Megillat Esther* and on Passover – '*peh*' (mouth) and '*saḥ*' (speaks) – we tell many stories of the Exodus from Egypt. There are many stories in our own lives. Each person has his own story, and all of our stories together are part of the story of our people, a story which is the greatest in all of human history.

"In the beginning, the story concerned our forefathers – Abraham, Isaac, Jacob, David; and now that story is about us. We all have our own story, and we can decide if we are the protagonist, the hero, or a secondary figure that the story passes by. Are you the leading figure in your story? Is your story a good story? Is your story connected to the story of the nation of Israel? Does your story advance our cause? Do you allow others to dominate your story? Are you genuinely free, or are you a slave to others or to your desires?"

Hadar did not yet know the vital role he was to play in our shared story.

The deeper meaning behind burning *ḥametz*

Passover Eve is full of stress. It is the culmination of detailed preparations, endless errands, and thorough cleaning. Twenty-four hours before sitting down at the Seder table, we search for *ḥametz*, burning it in the morning so that it is totally eradicated, while the main event, the big night, is still ahead of us. How can all the running around and last-minute preparations not lead to tension and short tempers? How can a large and diverse family reunion bring more joy than quarrels? This is, in fact, what we pray for. The prayer we recite while burning the *ḥametz* represents the ongoing effort to banish the evil inclination.

"May it be Your will, Hashem our God and God of our fathers, that You will have mercy on us and save us from consuming *ḥametz*, even the smallest amount, this year and every year throughout our lives, and just as we banished *ḥametz* from our homes and burned it, so may we merit to banish the evil inclination from within us always, all the days of our lives, and may we merit to cling to the desire to do good and to Your Torah, in order to fear You and love You always, we and our children and our children's children, may it be Your will."

Amen. *Ḥag Same'aḥ!*

THE PASSOVER HAGGADA
Seder night

Millions of Jews sit down each year around the Seder table and conduct the Seder according to the following order: *Kadesh* (say Kiddush), *Ureḥatz* (wash hands before eating *karpas*), *Karpas* (eat a vegetable), *Yaḥatz* (break the middle matza in two; set aside larger piece for the *afikoman*), *Maggid* (tell the Passover story), *Raḥtza* (wash hands before eating matza), *Motzi Matza* (eat the matza), *Maror* (eat bitter herbs), *Korekh* (eat a sandwich of matza and *maror*), *Shulḥan Orekh* (eat the festive meal), *Tzafun* (eat the *afikoman*), *Barekh* (recite Grace After Meals), *Hallel* (recite psalms of praise), *Nirtza* (pray that God accepts our mitzva).

Throughout history, there have been a multitude of inspired descriptions from our sages of what happens on this night. Here are a few simple but beautiful words for our time by Rabbi Chaim Navon:

"Seder night teaches us something profound about the nation of Israel, about the God of Israel, and about ourselves. It teaches us that we are not what we appear to be. The era of smartphones and social media deceive us into thinking that we are addicted to them, that we only care about what's new and what's cool, that we are restless partygoers, that our children are little tyrants who are hopelessly bored. Then suddenly on Seder night, between the jokes about matza and *ḥaroset* and complaints about the family being squashed together around the table, we discover who we really are: the children of Abraham, Isaac and Jacob, who yearn more than anything else to teach our children the secret of the eternal covenant, just as our parents taught it to us. We inwardly shed a tear when we are reminded of our grandparents, and another when we dream of our future grandchildren. Seder night around the table is kind of a mess, but in our minds it creates a perfect order." (Note: The Hebrew word for order is *seder*.)

"In great haste, we left Egypt"

In many North African communities, there is a custom to announce at the start of the Seder: "In great haste, we left Egypt." Would we ourselves, in the moment of truth, have left Egypt? Would we have understood the magnitude of the moment and jumped at the chance to get out? Passover teaches us the importance of not missing the moment. We could have missed this historic opportunity and remained slaves.

At the time of the British Mandate, Shlomo Ben Dahan organized illegal aliya from North Africa, mainly from Morocco. He and his associates devised an intricate plan to secretly anchor off the coast of a certain city and collect the Jews awaiting them to make the voyage to Israel. However, the nighttime navigation system mistakenly took them to a different coastal city in Morocco. What were they to do? Ben Dahan disembarked from the ship, knocked on the doors of Jews in the city in the middle of the night, and announced: "We arrived here by surprise. Our ship is anchored off the coast. In a few hours, the sun will rise and we will have to leave. Who is coming right now to the Land of Israel?"

What happened next was amazing: Within a few hours, many families boarded the ship, carrying with them the few possessions they had time to pack. The ship sailed for the Land of Israel full of new immigrants who recognized that they must not miss this chance to make aliya.

The story of the Exodus from Egypt teaches us to be alert and attentive to windows of opportunity that we encounter throughout our lives.

**"Let all who are hungry come and eat;
let all who are needy come and make Passover with us"**

As a child, the children's newspapers that I read included a popular column called "Test Yourself." After a series of questions, you discovered if you were miserly, organized, or friendly. Here is a "test yourself" for Seder night: Are you a slave or are you free?

The Seder opens with the following call: "Whoever is hungry, come eat with us." Rabbi Yosef Dov Soloveitchik, of blessed memory, who was one of the leaders of American Jewry, explained that this declaration is the essence of every Seder and every Exodus from slavery to freedom:

"The main aspect of freedom is sharing with someone else. A slave thinks only of himself, yet a free human being thinks of others and shares with them. The Seder symbolizes the birth of a community of kindness. It is a community of people who were only just released from bondage, emerging from isolation and focusing on themselves coming together as free people to create a community of kindness."

According to Rav Soloveitchik, this is a test for the entire year, not only for Seder night. Do you want to check if you are a slave or free? Ask yourself if you only care about yourself, or others too. This does not need to find expression in grand gestures. It can be as simple as washing dishes at the end of the Seder.

Rav Soloveitchik sees our engagement in spiritual content and discussion prior to the Seder meal as a great victory: "A human being should not regard hunger like an animal. A person can liberate the act of eating from being purely animalistic and transform it into a human practice built on free will and full of meaning. On this night, a person asks to redeem the activity of eating and make it holy."

"Why is this night different from all other nights?"

For many children, their first childhood memory of Passover is *"Ma nishtana"* ("Why is this night different?"), the moment they stand on a chair and sing the four questions. In a way, the questions on Passover are more important than the answers. Curiosity and the desire to learn are of greater consequence because without these it is impossible to progress and grow. This is why it is so important to involve the son "who does not know how to ask," and simply teach him to ask, to be intrigued and to overcome his indifference.

Professor Isidor Rabi, a Jewish American scientist who won the Nobel Prize in Physics, once explained the importance of asking questions. "All the mothers would ask their sons, 'Nu, what did you learn in school today?' but my mother always asked me a different question: 'Did you ask a good question today?' She taught me about asking good questions before she taught me about answering them."

"Whoever tells the story of the Exodus from Egypt at length deserves to be praised"

Besides the Holy Temple in Jerusalem, we have never invested in building impressive structures. Some cultures erect pyramids or statues to memorialize their past, but we have a different way of remembering: we tell our story. Rabbi Lord Jonathan Sacks explains the following:

"Three thousand years ago, Egypt and Israel were nations that asked themselves the most basic question: How do we defeat death? How do we become part of something that will endure when we are no longer here? The answer of the Egyptians has enthralled emperors and tyrants throughout history: we will prevail over mortality through building great monuments that will last for thousands of years. If we could go back through a time tunnel to the Egyptian pharaohs and tell them that their empire would

not survive and that those same Hebrew slaves, the children of
Israel, would survive, they would think that was absurd.

"The Jewish answer to this question was fundamentally
different: 'And you shall tell your child.' On the verge of obtaining their freedom, the children of Israel were told they would be
a nation of teachers. Freedom, Moses explained to them, is not
achieved on the battlefield or in the political arena. It requires families and schools in order to ensure that our ideals will be passed on
to the next generation and will never be lost. Moses understood
that a nation does not merit eternal life through building pyramids,
but rather through engraving values in the hearts of its children,
who will do the same with their children, and so on until the end
of time. The children of Israel built living monuments. They pre-
ferred words and instruction to stones, and did not see God as an
enslaving power but as a liberating force. Instead of worshiping
omnipotent rulers, they insisted on giving honor to the widow, the
orphan, the stranger, the vulnerable, the weak, and the neglected.
These were the values of our ancestors and we are their heirs."

This is what we have – a story. And whoever tells this story
at length deserves to be praised.

"It was regarding the four sons that the Torah spoke"

The segment of the four sons is one of the most famous in the
Haggada. "One is wise, one is wicked, one is simple, and one
doesn't even understand enough to ask questions." The accepted
commentary with which I was familiar explained that all four
have a place at the Seder table, and each one should be given an
opportunity to ask questions and to be answered in a manner fitting his level of understanding. There is even a parallel between
the four sons and the four species of Sukkot (lulav, etrog, myrtle,
willow), which represent the four kinds of Jews. (Note: The lulav
is from a date tree; the sweetness of its fruit represents someone with Torah knowledge. The myrtle is fragrant; its pleasant

aroma represents someone who does mitzvot and good deeds. The willow has neither taste nor fragrance and represents some- one without Torah or mitzvot. The etrog has both taste and fra- grance and represents someone who has Torah knowledge and also does mitzvot.)

However, the four sons can also be interpreted as repre- senting different states of mind within each one of us. There are times when we are wise, inquisitive, simply wanting to learn more; sometimes we can be wicked, not feeling part of the story at all; sometimes we can be simple and naive, not really understand- ing but still full of wonder and emotion; and sometimes we are the one who cannot even ask, in need of help to connect. "And these states of mind are to be found within every Jew," the *Sefat Emet* writes. In other words, these are voices that run through us throughout our lives, and we must make space for all of them and find appropriate responses so that we can continue in the spirit of the Seder and advance from slavery to freedom.

"One is wise, one is wicked, one is simple, and one doesn't understand enough to ask questions"

Seder night is designed to arouse curiosity in the younger genera- tion, and prompt children to ask questions. What do we do when faced with childish or confounding questions? How do we deal with questions that surprise us? A high school student who once prayed with the Rishon LeZion (leader of Sephardic Jewry in Israel), Rabbi Mordechai Eliyahu, told the following story:

"One day, our class took a trip to Jerusalem to pray Shaḥarit (morning prayers) with Rabbi Eliyahu, after which we accompa- nied him back to his home. It appeared that he was in a hurry to attend an event and his assistants tried to get us to move quickly in order not to delay him. Suddenly, from a distance, someone who appeared rather unbalanced approached the rabbi and began to shout, 'Rav Eliyahu, Rav Eliyahu!' The rabbi's assistants tried to hurry Rabbi Eliyahu along but he stopped, turned to the man shouting his name, and patiently asked what he wanted. This individual, with great seriousness, approached the rabbi and said, 'Honored Rav, I have a question: What blessing do we say before eating an apple?' This was as stupefying as if he had asked, 'Honored Rav, how do you make a cow?' A simple man like this approaching a rabbi as great as this with such an unnecessary question! But the rabbi did not laugh. He stopped, took his time, assumed the stance of someone deep in thought, and then answered as follows: 'Listen, that's a great question! You need to check and see if the apple is whole, in its natural state, and if so, then you bless, "Creator of the fruit of the tree." But perhaps the apple has been turned to a liquid and we are talking about apple juice, which requires a different blessing. Or perhaps the apple was cooked for dessert or made into applesauce. I suggest that you come to see me at the study hall so we can discuss this question in a serious manner….'

"The man became very emotional. He was excited that his question had received recognition and that importance had been placed on answering him. My friends and I, who had laughed at the expense of this bizarre neighbor, were forced to pause and consider what we had just witnessed. There are thousands of wonderful tales regarding Rabbi Eliyahu, but I am continually reminded of this story because of the care he took with every Jew, with every question, and with every apple."

"You shall tell your son"

Our Sages say that the word "Passover" can also mean "the mouth (*peh*) speaks (*saḥ*)." The obligation on this night is expressed in the words, "You shall tell your son." We must tell this story to ourselves, to each other, but primarily to our children. We are enjoined to speak, to loudly affirm our values and to talk at length about our heritage.

If Passover is the festival of freedom, then free speech marks the beginning of our liberation. I once interviewed a Syrian activist from the city of Idlib just after a bombardment. He interviewed openly, with his face uncovered, for the Israeli television station, but said that he feared Syrian President Assad and therefore could not tell me everything. I have also interviewed immigrants from the former Soviet Union. To this day, some of them find it difficult to speak freely, to adjust to a reality in which what they say is completely up to them and not limited by a totalitarian regime. From the days of Pharaoh until now, Passover calls upon us to liberate ourselves from the constraints of censored speech.

What should we speak about? What are we supposed to say? How can we utilize the power of free speech? Many nations have gained independence and a state of their own, only to quickly collapse from internal controversy and strife. The Haggada calls upon us to speak and act differently. The words spoken by the nation that went out from slavery to freedom are of an unerringly positive and grateful nature. The Seder is devoted to practicing how to express thanks, to give praise and extol Hashem. Beyond this, we are encouraged to pay attention to every word of the Haggada, since "whoever tells the story of the Exodus from Egypt at length deserves to be praised."

The Haggada does not only provide us with a factual historical account, but educates us to focus on the good that we see throughout history.

"And we shouted to Hashem, the God of our fathers, and Hashem heard our shouting, and He saw our suffering, our hard labor, and our oppression"

When was the last time you shouted? Not to other people, but to heaven? One of the words highlighted in the Haggada is *"Vanitzhak"* ("And we shouted"). This is when the redemption began, when the children of Israel understood that they were under duress and shouted out to God. At this point in the Seder, it is customary to offer prayers and make requests. Rabbi Shlomo Carlebach explained the meaning of "*Vanitzḥak*" as follows:

"Do you know why we are not truly happy? Because we live in a world where, from a certain age, it is forbidden to truly laugh, or truly cry, or truly shout. When children cry, they really cry! Friends, all I can tell you is this: When you want to cry, cry with your whole heart. Do you know how much better you will feel? Shout and weep before God. Know that your tears flow upward – they only seem to be streaming down, but really they are flowing up toward heaven."

Dayenu (**It would have been enough for us**)

Dayenu is not just a superficial cheery jingle to rouse the children. It is, in fact, a lesson for us all. It is a lesson about gratitude and focusing on the positive. We give thanks for every little thing that happened along the way; for the splitting of the Red Sea, we say, "It would have been enough," and also for the ten plagues, for the manna we ate in the desert, for the gift of Shabbat, for the Torah, for the Land of Israel, and so on. We are encouraged to always look at how full, and not how empty, our own glass happens to be.

During the Holocaust, Regina Honigman was a young prisoner in a forced labor camp in Gabersdorf. As Passover approached, she wrote a personal version of the Haggada in her diary. Her version of the four questions included poignant questions about her fate, and her description of bitter herbs referenced her own harsh ordeal in the labor camp, yet she kept her sense of humor. Her version of "*Dayenu*" went as follows: "Death, hunger – *dayenu*. Night arrives again – *dayenu*. There is a bed for the group leader – *dayenu*. When she feels like hitting us – *dayenu*. We do not care about getting slapped – *dayenu*. The group can laugh – *dayenu*."

Regina survived the Holocaust, and her family donated her diary to Yad Vashem, the World Holocaust Remembrance

Center. Her personal *"Dayenu"* perpetuates the inner message of the famous song. Even in the midst of evil, she searched and found some good over which to sing *"Dayenu."*

"In every generation, a person is obligated to see himself as if he personally had gone out of Egypt"

In the Tanya, the foundational work of the Chabad hasidic movement, there is a significant addition to this famous sentence: "In every generation – every single day – a person is obligated to see himself as if he personally had gone out of Egypt that day." Not only in every generation, but each and every day. What does this mean? The Tanya explains that this refers to the release of the divine soul from the confines of the body. In other words, our souls are still enslaved, and the Exodus from Egypt is not over. In fact, it continues every day, beginning again as we succeed in breaking bad habits to which we have been enslaved and progressing to higher levels of existence.

The Exodus from Egypt that we experienced yesterday is no longer sufficient. On the contrary, what was considered freedom only yesterday is considered Egyptian servitude today, and we must progress from this point. There is no limit to the pursuit of perfection.

Motzi Matza (blessing and eating the matza)

It is highly significant that our Sages called matza "the bread of faith." Every bite of matza brings not just calories to our system, but also faith inspired by the story of the Exodus from Egypt.

Eli Cohen was one of the most outstanding intelligence officers in our history. He spied for Israel in Damascus under a false identity, obtaining substantial invaluable information until he was caught and hanged. In recent years, his family received moving evidence of how he managed to acquire matza undercover in Damascus during Passover. Here is one account that his brother Avraham heard from a Jewish woman who made aliya from Syria:

"My father was a Jewish merchant in the Al-Hamidiyah shuk (open market) in Damascus. During Ḥol HaMoed (intermediate days) of Passover, a man calling himself Kamal Amin Thabet (Eli Cohen's fictitious name) entered our store. I was a little girl, but I remember how he approached my father and said, 'Mr. Yosef, I am very hungry. Do you have something to eat?' My father answered, 'Mr. Kamal, it is now Passover for us Jews. We have no bread or pita, only matza.' The distinguished visitor pretended that this was the first time he had heard of it. 'Matza? What is it? Okay, it doesn't matter. Bring me whatever you have – the main thing is to eat something.' I remember how Eli Cohen took the matza in his hands, went into a corner, mumbled a few words quietly to himself, and ate it."

In memory of the heroic Eli Cohen,
who even in the most difficult and dangerous circumstances
did not forget the "bread of faith."

Shulḥan Orekh (the Seder meal)

I was once invited to speak at a diplomatic gathering several days before Passover. Dozens of foreign ambassadors to Israel had been invited to a Tel Aviv hotel. The purpose was to explain the holiday to them. The Russian ambassador did not understand why everyone was so obsessed with cleaning at this time, and the Ethiopian ambassador did not understand the significance of the matza that everyone would be eating.

They sat at a table with a Seder plate placed before them, but I thought it was less important to explain the meaning of the different items on the plate, the symbols, and the customs, than it was to convey the essence of Passover. I pointed out that whereas usually, when we want to learn about a subject, we gather in a lecture hall for a day of speeches and discussions, or we read a book of articles on that subject, on Seder night, we learn the meaning of Passover sitting at a table that is laden with food. Why is that? I explained that on the night that we commemorate leaving Egypt, we do not just speak about our values, but eat them. We do not just speak about freedom, but drink it. We do not lecture about equality, but sing it. On this night, we disseminate our values with the crumbs of matza, imbibe them with sips of wine, and hide them with the afikoman, which the children search for and find. Jewish tradition does not just talk about values – it lives them too.

"Who Knows One? I Know One!"

At first glance, this is just a nice children's song. How did it become such a significant part of the Seder? According to one explanation, "Who Knows One?" is an association game, a personal test. We have been through a process during the Seder, and now we are checking to see if we have absorbed the messages. What associations do we make? Does the number one remind us of the first day of the month, the day on which our salary is deposited into our bank account? Does the number two remind us of who came in second in our party's primary elections? And the number four, does that bring to mind a four-by-four Jeep? Does the number twelve remind us of the twelve-month warranty on our new washing machine? This song checks our mindset after a night of education. The importance of the number four relates to the number of our matriarchs; twelve, above all, is the number of Israel's tribes. All the components of our identity are defined within this song, and it should come naturally to us to relate them as such by the time Seder night comes to a close.

SHEVI'I SHEL PESAḤ (SEVENTH DAY OF PASSOVER)

Imagining the impossible

On Seder night, at the beginning of Passover, we celebrate the Exodus from Egypt. On the seventh day of Passover, the last day of the festival, we celebrate the splitting of the Red Sea. Rabbanit Yemima Mizrachi asks us to try to imagine what the crossing of the Red Sea was like:

"On the seventh day of Passover, a strong wind began to blow, and before the astonished eyes of the children of Israel and the Egyptians, something occurred that no one would have believed could happen: The sea split. It split! Yes, it is possible. And so you take one step, and then another and another until you reach the other side. Meanwhile, you leave all your misery and suffering behind, including the enemy soldiers who are chasing you. As you imagine this scene, you suddenly feel an irrepressible desire to sing *Shirat HaYam*, the Song of the Sea, and to imagine it like a painting. You see yourself crossing to the other side, your children clutching your dress, not believing what they have just witnessed. You have just passed between transparent walls of water and find yourself on the road to freedom.

"From time to time, each of us needs a splitting of the Red Sea when it comes to our livelihood, health, education, or marriage, as we embrace a new reality when it comes to our personal, community, or national circumstances. This was possible then and it is possible now. We need only believe that it is possible to change reality and also to change ourselves. We can emerge on the other side of the sea, transitioning from the straits to an expansive and limitless life."

When the sea split

What is the significance of the sea becoming dry land? I heard the following explanation from Yoel Cohen, a leading Chabad rabbi, paraphrased as follows:

The revealed and the hidden worlds confuse us. Most of the time, the truth is hidden beneath a sea of pretty images, brands, and lies. Whoever is rich or beautiful, well spoken or famous is considered successful. We do not pay attention to those who are less ostentatious or not in the public eye, and we do not appreciate them. They are off to the side, hidden. But who determined that it must be so? Who says that we know how to properly evaluate success or distinguish between what is true and what is false?

The miracle of the Exodus from Egypt was that for one instant, we saw the world as it really is. What is normally hidden became clear before our very eyes. The nation of Israel reached a very high level of perception, with no restriction, obscurity, or disguise. The nation understood the spiritual way in which the world works behind the scenes. It is said that even a maidservant who was present at the splitting of the sea saw and perceived more than the prophet Ezekiel in his vision of the divine chariot. Yes, to that remarkable extent. This is also the deeper meaning of the Exodus from Egypt – to remind us that sometimes, the world we see is upside down and confusing, and we must strive to reveal what is hidden beneath the surface.

Open your eyes

The splitting of the Red Sea was inconceivable. Today we celebrate the miracle of the waters parting and the children of Israel crossing over on dry land. Yet, in the midst of this remarkable event, two Jews found reason to grumble. They complained to each other about the mess, the water, the sand. Our Sages described this scenario as follows:

"There were two men, Reuven and Shimon, who grumbled among the Israelites. As they walked through the sea, all they could talk about was the mud. Reuven said: 'In Egypt, we had mud, and now in the sea we have mud. In Egypt, we had clay for bricks, and here too, we have an abundance of clay to make bricks.' They rebelled at the sea, even though this was the parting of the

Red Sea! They didn't notice the water; they only saw the mud"
(Exodus Rabba 24:1).

This is a catastrophic mindset. These two men are about to
walk right through the middle of the Red Sea, but they do not even
notice the many miracles happening around them. The awareness
that they are transitioning from slavery to freedom is lost on them,
so preoccupied are they with comparisons and complaints, seeing
only small details rather than the big picture.

The poet Yehuda Amichai describes this incident in his
poem, aptly titled "Miracles":

"From afar, everything looks like a miracle / but up close,
not even a miracle looks like one / Even someone who crossed
the Red Sea when the waters split / saw only the sweaty back of
the person in front of him / and the swaying of his big thighs."

Our commentators call upon us to pay attention to this
phenomenon, and to learn the lesson of those who complained in
the midst of the miracle of the Red Sea. We need to open our eyes
and look up. We must not be so busy criticizing and complaining
that we confuse moments of joy and redemption with moments
of slavery. Instead, we should recognize and acknowledge all the
good in our lives in the present moment, expressing gratitude for
the miracles taking place all around us.

MIMOUNA

What is Mimouna?

At the end of Passover, Jews from Morocco traditionally celebrate
Mimouna. It is an evening of sumptuous dining tables, traditional
clothes, and sweet delicacies – especially mofletta, a crepe filled
with honey, jam, fruit, or nuts. What is the reason for this celebration?

- Mimouna comes from the word *"emuna"* (faith). It is the
  culmination of the journey that began on Seder night,

through the intermediate festival days, and finally, the last day of the festival, as we reaffirm our faith in our future redemption that will surely come.

- After a week of seclusion, the Jewish community in Morocco would buy back the *ḥametz* it had sold to its Muslim neighbors before Passover, and Mimouna became a celebration of the first opportunity to bake with it.

- During Mimouna, it was (and still is) customary to leave the front door open, in order to increase the mitzva of welcoming guests. After a week in which everyone was diligent about keeping a kosher Passover kitchen, and people may have avoided eating in each other's homes due to differences in customs, this night symbolized renewed feelings of closeness and brotherhood. Each family visited their neighbors to partake of their dishes and wish them *"Tirbeḥu vetisadu"* (good luck and success).

- Many Israelis of Moroccan heritage oppose what Mimouna has become in Israel today. It has turned into an occasion for politicians' visits and barbecues in public parks that do not reflect the essence of the day. In Morocco, it was also a day for giving *tzedaka*, learning Torah, and gathering for special prayers.

The holiday of faith

Many events took place on Zoom during the pandemic, including a Mimouna. Here is Miriam Peretz's address given during a Zoom Mimouna at the end of Passover 5780 (2020):

"Mimouna calls upon us to move a single part of our bodies that perhaps we have not moved enough in the past. We have moved our arms and legs a lot during visits to the malls. Our eyes have moved plenty too, looking around all the stores. But one body part we have not moved enough is our heart. Now, thank God, this is happening. The more rules we are given about distancing ourselves from each other, with reminders to maintain a space of two meters, the closer our hearts become. During Mimouna, our doors are open and our homes are full. This year our doors are closed; what can we do? Let us focus on what remains open: the heart. Our hearts are open this year more than ever.

"During Passover, I thought to myself: How did the children of Israel simply walk into the Red Sea? Weren't they afraid that the water would cover them? The answer is: they had '*mimouna*.' Mimouna is *emuna* (faith). They had faith that they would succeed. This is the essence of Mimouna, celebrated on the day after Passover. Above all, faith is the capacity to know that there is hope, that you will emerge from the sea, that evil decrees will be rescinded, that we will get through the pandemic and celebrate many more happy occasions. And faith is especially tested during a time of crisis.

"Why did Miriam, the sister of Moses, take a tambourine with her when she left Egypt? When people run away, they quickly take what is important and can easily be carried. Since when does someone running away take a tambourine? The answer is that Miriam's tambourine symbolized faith, the knowledge that it would all turn out for the best, that we would prevail and there would be much to celebrate, that everything promised to us would come to pass. During this period, we must all seek our own 'Miriam's tambourine,' our own faith. This is our most important resource. *Tirbeḥu vetisadu* (good luck and success)."

RETURNING TO ROUTINE
Touch down

Rabbi Shlomo Wolbe used to say that not only is the festival itself important, so too is the transition back to ordinary life. He compared it to a spaceship returning to the earth's atmosphere. It is well known that this is a very sensitive point in the journey due to the enormous heat generated during this transition. We too must pay attention to how we navigate back into our routine, with all the spiritual cargo we accumulated during the holiday.

Are you familiar with the custom of building a sukka immediately after Yom Kippur in order to channel the exalted feelings of Yom Kippur into a practical activity? This mechanism can assist us now as well. Can we search for a practical way to express the positive longings that are vibrating within us? Something that will continue the Exodus from slavery to freedom in our gray, everyday routine. We could, for example, schedule a daily time for learning something new in Torah, or make and follow through on a commitment to improve our character. Any change, big or small, can serve as a vessel into which we pour the spiritual abundance we feel after the Passover holiday so that we make the most of it and ensure we don't lose it.

SEFIRAT HAOMER (COUNTING THE OMER)
Trusting the process

On the night following the Seder, with the beginning of Ḥol HaMoed (intermediate festival days) in Israel, we begin to count the Omer.

At the conclusion of evening prayers throughout the Omer, we recite the following blessing: "Blessed are You, Lord our God, King of the universe, who has sanctified us by His commandments and commanded us concerning the counting of the Omer," and then count the current day of the Omer. This continues for seven weeks, day after day, until the forty-ninth day, bringing us to the day before Shavuot, the festival commemorating the giving of the Torah on Mount Sinai.

There is a striking contrast between the seminal event that we celebrate on Seder night and the counting that begins the next night, between the "wow" of the Seder and the mundanity of the small details that follow.

There are profound, mystical meanings that inform this period, but first and foremost, counting the Omer is simply a process, and that is the lesson we can learn: to trust in the process.

Seven weeks elapse between leaving Egypt and receiving the Torah, as we emerge from slavery to freedom. During this time, there is a road that must be traveled, a process to undergo. In an era in which we lose our patience if it takes more than a few seconds for a WhatsApp message to send, who among us is prepared to wait a full seven weeks for something to happen and, in the meantime, progress one small step at a time each day?

May you find fulfillment in the process. Happy counting!

I am here

Rabbi Yoni Lavi writes: "Four hundred years ago, Shakespeare poignantly asked, 'To be or not to be?' The modern era gives a surprising answer to this question: To be and not to be – both at the same time. Many of us choose not to be truly present, even when we appear to be. We are always available to everyone. We are perpetually on 'vibrate.' Not our phones, but us. We are everywhere at once, yet we are nowhere.

"The mitzva of *Sefirat HaOmer* that we observe during this period offers another way of being. Just before we perform the daily count, we stop and declare: 'I am here and ready to fulfill the positive mitzva of counting the Omer.' There are those who declare their presence and readiness before performing each mitzva, but before counting the Omer, this declaration has become, for many, part of the mitzva itself. It takes only a few seconds to say these few words, but they allow us to focus. To prepare ourselves. To silence the vibrations. We make ourselves available exclusively for this moment because it will not come again. We are simply present, completely.

"If we wish, this mindset can be adopted in other areas of our life, such as interactions with our spouse, bedtime stories with our

children, our daily prayers, and time spent alone with ourselves.
I am here and ready. I am truly present."

Ethical behavior precedes receiving the Torah

There is a common practice that begins on the Shabbat following
Passover and continues into the summer months: studying one
chapter of *Pirkei Avot* (Ethics of the Fathers) every Shabbat afternoon. *Pirkei Avot* is a talmudic tractate that addresses morality
and virtues rather than law and halakha. It is said that "*derekh eretz
kadma laTorah*," ethical behavior precedes receiving or studying
the Torah. In this spirit, we learn about ethical behavior during
the counting of the Omer as we approach the giving of the Torah
on the festival of Shavuot.

Here are several revolutionary definitions from *Pirkei Avot*
(4:1) that explain the meaning of true wisdom, strength, wealth,
and honor.

> "Who is wise? He who learns from every person.
> Who is strong? He who conquers his evil inclination.
> Who is rich? He who is happy with what he has.
> Who is honored? He who honors others."

Each one of these wise maxims shatters our perception of success,
and requires us to work on our own inner sense of these values.

Two more worthy examples include: "Let the honor of
your fellow be as dear to you as your own" (2:10), and "Welcome
every person with a cheerful countenance" (1:15). Perhaps these
thoughts sound like pleasant clichés from kindergarten, but
once a year we are called upon to study them again, regardless
of how old we are, and try to build a society that is founded on
these noble values.

YOM HASHOAH – HOLOCAUST MARTYRS' AND HEROES' REMEMBRANCE DAY

The lowest of lows and the highest of highs

In Israel, the twenty-sixth of Nisan has been designated as Holocaust Martyrs' and Heroes' Remembrance Day (Yom HaShoah). The following was written by Rabbi Professor Eliezer Berkovits, who published testimonies of the victims' adherence to Torah and good deeds under impossible circumstances. Berkovits claims that the Holocaust, above all else, highlights the free choice that a person has between good and evil:

"In no other place and at no other time in history has it been possible to test the absurdity of existence as it was in the German extermination camps. By the same token, it is also true that in no other place and at no other time in history has it been possible to experience such an elevated existence. The two are intertwined. In Auschwitz and in Treblinka, in the camps and in the ghettos, the perpetrators could descend into the depths of depravity. At the same time there were those who rose to the greatest heights of honor and virtue. The story of the descent of man is well known. Yet, perhaps because of our grief for him, we have not given sufficient attention to man's greatness."

This is an important point when remembering and learning about the Holocaust: along with grappling with the horror and sheer evil of it, we must recognize the humanity, the nobility, and the devotion to doing good that were also revealed. Or, as Rabbi Berkovits says, we must give more prominence to those who managed to force humanity on hell.

Honoring the survivors

A disturbing phenomenon has been occurring in recent years in the media coverage on Yom HaShoah: there appears to be a preoccupation with the economic hardship experienced by Holocaust survivors, rather than focusing on the Holocaust itself. The welfare of the survivors is of course an important topic for any day, but why devote so much time to it on this day in particular? Maybe it is an easy escape from the many significant issues raised by the destruction of one-third of the Jewish nation. Should the Israeli bureaucracy and the Ministry of Finance be the central subject of the day?

Dr. Moti Shalem, who founded the International School for Holocaust Studies at Yad Vashem, wrote the following: "The story of Holocaust survivors in Israel is not a story of misery, poverty, and neglect. It is a story of phenomenal success, of amazing rehabilitation, of choosing life, of establishing families and building the nation in the Land of Israel. This is what needs to be told on Yom HaShoah. Poverty and the childless elderly need to be cared for daily throughout the year, but it does not need to be the focus this week. Abba Kovner said of the generation of survivors: 'It wouldn't surprise me if they became a band of robbers, thieves, and murderers; even then, they would probably still be the most humane and just people the world has ever known.'"

Let us mark this day with respect, and in doing so, honor the survivors in the way they deserve.

One more memory

Esther Farbstein is a historian, researcher, and founder and head of the Center for Holocaust Studies at Michlalah Jerusalem College. She is also the wife of Rabbi Moshe Mordechai Farbstein, head of the Hebron Yeshiva in Jerusalem. In her research, she often describes responses to dilemmas faced by observant Jews during the Holocaust. Could you eat nonkosher meat when no other food was available? Under forced labor conditions, how do you violate Shabbat in the most minimal way? What do you say to a boy who does not think he will reach bar mitzva age and wants to put tefillin on early? We see from her research that heroism was displayed not only by partisans, but by all those who secretly lit Hanukka candles.

This is the mindset that Farbstein suggests that we, the next generation, would be wise to adopt: "We are all familiar with private memories. Every family has them, and we honor them by naming our children after loved ones who have passed away and mourning on the anniversary of their deaths. This is, of course, important. We also understand community memory – in fact, whole communities in Israel are named in memory of communities that were destroyed in Europe. And we need public memories as well. Public memories are the values that we want to carry forward for future generations.

"As yet, there have been two types of public memory, but it is time to add a third. First, there is the Zionist public memory that speaks about nationalism and Hebrew might. The lesson from the Holocaust is that we must be independent and strong in the face of threat. This was once the dominant approach. Today, another approach is developing, and that is the universal approach: the Holocaust teaches that we need to fight racism, hatred of the other, and the existence of evil. This is all well and good, but it is not enough. All nations, without a doubt, certainly need to draw conclusions about fighting evil, but is this the principle message for us, the descendants of the murdered? Does the entire lesson concern how we should relate to the Palestinians, as the radical left sometimes claims?

"It must be said that the Holocaust was a Jewish event, and the lesson the Jewish people should learn from it is to not only be better people in general, but also to be better Jews. Along with the Zionist memory and the universal memory, we have a grave responsibility to formulate a Jewish public memory as well: we must strengthen the Jewish people from the inside, from within its values. The Nazis fought against our Judaism, and the more we strengthen our Jewish identity, the more we will honor the memory of those who perished."

The survivors, too, are holy

My grandmother Ada Rosenstrauch, of blessed memory, was a Holocaust survivor. She was born in Piotrkow, Poland, survived the Bergen-Belsen camp, and passed away at the age of ninety-four. She worked as a physical education teacher until a very advanced age, full of strength and a source of inspiration. After losing many of her relatives in the *Shoah*, Grandma Ada made aliya to Israel, settled in Haifa, married my grandfather, and raised my father and his siblings.

"You shall sanctify yourselves and be holy, for I am Hashem, your God" (Lev. 20:7). This is written in the Torah portion of *Kedoshim* that is read at this time of year. What is holiness? We are used to speaking about the six million souls who perished in the Holocaust as holy, but there was also great holiness in the resolution of the survivors to cling to life.

This is the meaning of *Kaddish* – "*Yitgadal veyitkadash Shemei rabba*" (Exalted and hallowed be His great Name). In other words, after a loss, we must continue to exalt life and the presence of the Creator in our world, to sanctify reality. Today, when people tragically lose family members, an entire nation cares for them with compassion and love. All of us embrace them, as in the case of Tamar Fogel, whose parents and three siblings were murdered in a terrorist attack in Itamar, or in the case of the four Henkin children, who saw their parents murdered while traveling with them in the family van, among many other such tragic cases.

Yet, an entire generation of Holocaust survivors, orphans who lost parents, siblings, and homes, found themselves coping alone, without any attention, much less the embrace of an entire nation. Millions of survivors resolved to rise from the ruins, to build and create, to believe, to persevere, to give birth, and to study and plant and love. This is an unmatched historical feat. It was a rebuke to the evil and depravity that the survivors had endured, a determination to add goodness and holiness to the world. There-fore, in a sense, the survivors, among them my grandma Ada, of blessed memory, are holy too.

Carrying the legacy

A few days before Yom HaShoah 5779 (2019), Rabbi Menachem Taub, the Rebbe of Kaliv, passed away at the age of ninety-six. He was a Holocaust survivor who had been severely tortured and was not able to have children of his own, but he merited to educate many with this message: remember and never forget. Here are three ideas that he used to repeat often over the years:

- "There was a king who built a magnificent palace. When his son succeeded him, he built a palace even more spectacu-lar than his father's. When the grandson was crowned, he said: 'I am unworthy of building a palace more glorious than my grandfather's and my father's. Yet what am I capa-ble of doing? I will clean the dust that has gathered on their palaces so that everyone will be reminded of their glory.' So we too must care for and protect the palaces of our an-cestors. We perpetuate their legacy."

- "We ourselves may be Holocaust deniers. If we do not re-member the Holocaust every day and do nothing to per-petuate memories of it, we are in denial. Whoever has tes-timonies, diaries, or pictures and does not bring them to the attention of the world performs a great injustice to the memories of the holy ones who perished."

- In the camps, we were beaten for no reason other than be-cause we were Jews. And here we have been privileged to come to the Land of Israel and redeem its soil. Why do we argue over petty politics? Only through love and brother-hood will we merit, through the kindness of Hashem, to be redeemed quickly and to welcome the righteous Messiah."

Know how to say "I don't know"

To be a believer does not mean you have an automatic explanation for everything. Indeed, the opposite is true. A believer also has many questions and concerns. You see the change of fortunes throughout history and they are not always clear and unambiguous.

In his book *B'Netivot HaEmuna*, Rabbi Tzvi Markovitz, a member of the Council of Torah Sages and a rabbi in Ramat Gan writes, "Meanings are hidden. The prophetic lament that foretells the destruction of the Holy Temple is a Megilla called '*Eikha*' (known as Lamentations; translates literally as 'How'). Its central theme is a large, pending question mark: How could such an event possibly take place? How could this happen? How did the nation of Israel reach such a state that divine oversight obligated the Temple's destruction? So too, the *megillot* (stories) of destruction in our own time begin and end with '*Eikha*.' The Holocaust is a vast lamentation in which every letter is red with the blood of millions, scorched from the fires of the crematoria. How could this have taken place? How could this happen?"

The Holocaust causes us to ask "*Eikha*?" Rabbi Markovitz reaches many fascinating conclusions about the Holocaust in his book, but does not push aside a sense of catastrophic devastation and wonder, an inability to understand – and yet keeping an ultimate belief and trust in God.

Knowing which note to use

Rabbi Yehoshua Moshe Aaronson lost his wife and children in the Holocaust. After the war, he provided much assistance to refugees, made aliya to Petah Tikva, and started a new family. Where did he find the strength to build all over again, to move forward? Rabbi Aaronson demanded this not only of himself but of his entire generation. In one of his books he quotes the famous hasidic saying that each person should carry two notes in his pocket. On one slip of paper he should write, "I am dust and ashes." The other should say, "The world was created for me." These two quotes express opposite states of being. Sometimes a person needs to be "dust and ashes," to be humble, low, and submissive, and sometimes a person needs to feel that the world was created for him, to strengthen himself, to elevate himself, to act with confidence.

It is important, however, to know when to use each slip of paper, because people tend to get confused: to humble themselves instead of taking action, or to make a spectacle of themselves when it would be preferable to keep quiet. "My generation was a generation of 'I am dust and ashes,'" Rabbi Aaronson said. "We reached the lowest point; we became like dust. Now we need to focus on the second note with all our strength. Presently, our task is to strengthen ourselves with the message that 'the world was created for me.' Nation of Israel: let us rise up and renew ourselves in the land of our hearts' desire!"

In other words, our mission, that of the generations after the Holocaust, is to fill the vacuum and not be ashamed to spread our wings and dream big. We must rise up from tragedy and build a secure Jewish alternative with strength, in the midst of a world that failed us.

Knowledge is power

We hear countless personal stories about the Holocaust that are emotionally gripping, but we must not neglect the cold, hard facts. Professor Yosef Ben-Shlomo, the notable philosopher and teacher, prepared a list of six historical facts that we need to internalize in order to understand why the Holocaust was such a unique event:

1. *Judenrein*: For the first time in history (other than Haman's plot against the Jews in ancient Persia), one nation sought the complete annihilation of another, despite the fact that the vast majority of the nation targeted for extermination lived outside the territory of the aggressor nation. The goal

was not just to exile the other nation, but to erase it from the face of the earth. In Nazi documents on the number of Jews destined for death, even the tiny Albanian Jewish community of two hundred souls was counted.

2. Absence of opposition: At the Wannsee Conference of January 1942, the "Final Solution" was unanimously approved by the fifteen attendees, all of whom held high-ranking ministerial positions in the German government, and eight of whom were holders of doctorate degrees. Not one stood in opposition.

3. The Germans worked against their own interests in World War II. Even as Germany was losing the war, it behaved irrationally. Instead of investing in just fighting enemy forces, the Germans continued to "waste" their energy on their Jewish extermination project.

4. They were not crazy. Among the murderers were family men and women, professionals, and intellectuals. They were perfectly sane. Millions of ordinary, regular folks did not see any problem with taking part in this giant extermination project.

5. The concentration camps were not bombed. The death factories continued to operate without interference by the Western allied nations or their armies, even while the Allies regularly bombed Nazi munitions factories.

6. There was no way out. Unlike their ability to cope with other horrendous decrees and persecutions throughout history, the Jews of Europe had no way out. There was no possibility of saving themselves through cooperation with the enemy or by being exiled, or by conversion to another faith. Death was the only option that awaited them.

Today we face Holocaust denial, ignorance, and disregard, as well as claims that the Holocaust was not a unique or particularly anti-Jewish event. It is therefore more important than ever to remember the facts of what happened – knowledge is power.

Iyar

YOM HAZIKARON – MEMORIAL DAY FOR ISRAEL'S FALLEN SOLDIERS AND VICTIMS OF TERRORISM
The first casualty of our return to the Land of Israel

The fourth of Iyar, the day before Independence Day, is Memorial Day for those killed in action in the IDF, in underground militias prior to the founding of the state, in the Mossad (Israeli Secret Intelligence Service), and in the Shin Bet (Israel Security Agency). It also memorializes those killed in hostile enemy and terrorist attacks. Each year memorial services are held, Israeli flags are lowered to half-mast, and a siren is sounded at 11 a.m., when all traffic comes to a halt and everyone stands for a moment of silence.

Each year, the total number of casualties is noted, a figure that is now more than twenty thousand, but when did we begin to count? Who was the first casualty? The first victim of a hostile enemy attack was Rabbi Avraham Shlomo Zalman Tzoref, who was murdered in 5611 (1851). The count does not begin with the War of Independence, but much earlier, with the renewal of the Jewish settlement in Jerusalem.

Rabbi Tzoref was born in Lithuania. He made aliya with his wife and three children, together with more than five hundred students of the Vilna Gaon, who immigrated to Israel between

5568–5570 (1808–1810). Rabbi Tzoref was a Torah scholar and a public figure who made his living as a silversmith, from which his family name was derived ("silversmith" is *"tzoref"* in Hebrew). He quickly became a highly visible leader. Rabbi Tzoref traveled to Egypt to obtain permission from the governing authorities to rebuild the destroyed Hurva Synagogue in the Jewish Quarter of Jerusalem's Old City. He was successful and the synagogue was inaugurated with much fanfare, while religious and welfare institutions were established around it. There was no limit to the rabbi's creative efforts to attract funds, to develop Jerusalem, and to bring more immigrants to Israel. This success angered some of the city's Arabs, and they tried to assassinate him. The first time, the shooter missed his mark, but the second time, on the rabbi's way to morning prayers at the synagogue he had rebuilt, several Arabs assaulted him and stabbed him with a sword. He survived for ten months until he passed away on the nineteenth of Elul 5611 (1851). On his deathbed, he recited the *Shema* and made his children swear that they would never leave the Land of Israel.

In the course of time, Rabbi Tzoref would be recognized as the first victim of terrorism in the Land of Israel during modern times, and this distinction was immortalized on a plaque on Mount Herzl. His family continued the legacy of settling the land and learning Torah. His grandson, Yoel Moshe Salomon, was among the founders of Petah Tikva. His family has a file of all the names of his descendants, which number more than twenty-three thousand.

Seen in historical perspective, Rabbi Tzoref was murdered in 1851, nine years before the birth of Theodore Herzl in 1860. Our story of the modern settlement of the Land of Israel is older than it might seem.

Don't stop living

After two of Aaron's sons perish at the inauguration of the *Mishkan* (desert Sanctuary), Moses hears a short message from God with which he consoles Aaron: "I will be sanctified through those close to Me" (Lev. 10:3). It is customary to interpret the phrase to mean that the Creator takes those who are closest and holiest for Himself, or as we say, "God takes the good ones," an expression I have sadly heard all too often at funerals.

The Rashbam, Rabbi Shmuel Ben Meir, wrote that we need to understand God's words to Moses in a different way. He explains that those close to God are not the ones who have died, but instead it is those who remain, who must overcome the loss, and continue to live and to build. The Rashbam writes that this is the message to Aaron the High Priest who lost his sons: "Do not mourn and do not cry, and do not desist from your service." In other words, continue what you are doing, your positive activity and your service as a priest, and do not allow death to interrupt life.

The Rashbam wrote this commentary a thousand years ago in France, but his words are appropriate even today for grieving families who sanctify life through their insistence on continuing to work, to live, and to thrive.

Closer to real life

Ruti Fogel, her husband Rabbi Ehud Fogel, and three of their children were murdered in a terrorist attack in the town of Itamar in 5771 (2011). Since then, Ruti's parents, Tali and Rabbi Yehuda Ben Yishai, have raised their three children who survived. At one of the Memorial Day ceremonies, I listened to Tali give a short speech that was moving and thought-provoking.

"I realized very quickly that our loss was huge, but that I must not stop myself from seeing that what I still had was even greater. Yes, I should allow myself to cry with crazy longings, but after crying, I should express gratitude over and over again for Ruti and Udi's wonderful children who live with us, who with God's help, will grow up and mature with unique strength and qualities. I understood that I have to live in both worlds: I have to live in this world with full force – to cook, to organize, to shop, to plant flowers. But I also live in the next world. How? By knowing that there are challenges that I must overcome, while maintaining values such as doing good, being honest, and having a higher purpose. By understanding that I am here in this world and must take advantage of every minute. And by knowing that there is such a thing as *teḥiyat hametim* (resurrection of the dead), which is not some kind of faraway, elusive vision. Revival of the dead means not allowing them to expire. Those of us who are here in this world bring them to life all the time. Our very existence, the fact that we are here, keeps their spirit alive.

"Sacrifices – this is what we usually call those who are killed in order to sanctify God's name. Ruti and Udi were not killed because the terrorists wanted to attack them personally, but because they wanted to attack the people of Israel. Yes, they were victims (*korbanot*), but that word is also associated with being close (*karov*), and bringing closer (*kiruv*). They were not the only victims; those of us who remain here carrying a tremendous burden are also *korbanot*. We feel differently, and do not concern ourselves so much with little things. We too are victims, but what we sacrificed does not lead us to despair, to give up on life. Rather, we are victims who feel close – close to our loved ones who have gone to a world that is all good. We are close to those in distress, those experiencing difficulties, and closer to real life."

Don't perpetuate tragedy

Rabbi Aharon Goldberg is the grandson of Rabbi Shlomo Zalman Auerbach, of blessed memory. He is among the leading halakhic authorities in our generation. He once attended an event in Yad Binyamin, where many former residents of Gush Katif (in the Gaza Strip) had lived before their expulsion in 2005. In the course of his remarks, he shared a major principle regarding memory and loss, revival and rebuilding:

"When I arrived here, the name 'Yad Binyamin' jumped out at me. Many of you have experienced tragedy. You were forced to leave your home and your community. In the Torah it is written that Binyamin was born as his mother, Rachel, passed away, and Rachel requested that they call him Ben Oni, meaning 'son of my affliction' (Gen. 35:18). Despite this, his father Jacob called him Binyamin (in English, Benjamin, 'son of the right' or 'son of the strong hand,' a name with a positive connotation). My grandfather asked: Why did Jacob not heed Rachel's last wish? The answer, he told us, was that we do not need to immortalize tragedy. Yes, a tragedy happened, and Rachel called her son Ben Oni during a difficult time, but people need to move forward. With all the grief and pain of his mother's tragic death, the child would still have to grow up. Therefore, Jacob chose the name Binyamin. There is in this name some memory of the tragedy, but there was no need to perpetuate the tragedy in the way it would have been with the name Ben Oni. When I entered your community and saw the name 'Yad Binyamin,' I said to myself: You too remember, but you are moving forward, making progress. It is always necessary to remember, but it is equally necessary to grow from our memories."

It's not just a news story; it's a learning experience

Over the years, I have interviewed, sadly, dozens of grieving families. You stand outside the door knowing that the family inside has just lost a loved one, and ask yourself: Are you making it easier on them by coming, or are you just irritating them? You ask them if they want to be interviewed and sometimes they refuse, but call you back a month later and say, "Now we do."

Once, after leaving a heartbreaking funeral on Mount Herzl, a family member approached me and asked to receive a copy of the video that was filmed. I gave her the phone number of the archives department of the news station and said, without thinking, that bereaved families are immediately sent copies of the videos taken of them. She stopped, looked at me, and the following words slowly rolled off of her tongue: "Bereaved family. You are the first person to say this to me. From now on, we are a bereaved family."

But this job is not only sad, and I am sure other journalists would agree with me. It is difficult, of course, but it is also full of meaning. Alongside coverage of the victims of war and terrorism, there are always the typical headline stories concerning political intrigue or suspected leaks from a sensitive inquiry. In the midst of these daily new stories, suddenly, family members of the deceased are being interviewed, and it changes the perspective for everyone watching or listening. One interview with a victim's family can remind us of the bigger picture of the Jewish people, a story of which we are all a part, and just a few words from them can remind us what really matters and prompt us to hug our children just a little tighter when they get home. This is not news coverage, it is life lessons.

YOM HAATZMA'UT – INDEPENDENCE DAY
Vibrations of holiness

On the fifth of Iyar, 5708 (1948), the British Mandate in this region came to an end and the State of Israel was established. Our generation may take our country for granted, not understanding that it is deserving of special appreciation, but whoever was here in 1948 will never see it that way.

Moshe Yekutiel Alpert, a *haredi* Jew who lived in the old settlement of Jerusalem prior to statehood, was the "*mukhtar*" or unofficial leader, of several Jerusalem neighborhoods. In his diary, he describes going to vote for the first Knesset after the establishment of the state. The words he wrote lend a proper perspective to our more mundane concerns:

"At 05:35, early in the morning, I got up with my wife, my brother Reb Shimon Leib, my brother-in-law Reb Netanel Saldovin, and my son Dov. After we drank coffee, we donned Shabbat clothes in honor of this great and holy day, as it says, 'This is the day that Hashem made; we will exult and rejoice in it' (Ps. 118:24). For two thousand years of exile, it could even be said that since the six days of Creation, we have never had the privilege to experience a day such as this – to vote in elections in a Jewish state, and to recite the blessing: 'Blessed be the One Who granted us life, sustained us, and enabled us to reach this occasion.'

"My son Dov left the house at 05:45 and stayed out all day and all night because he is a strong supporter of the Etzel [Jewish underground militia during the British Mandate period] list of candidates. Then I, my wife, my brother, and brother-in-law went to the polling station in the area of HaChabashim Street, with our State of Israel identity cards in hand. We walked the short distance with tremendous joy, and all along the way, I danced as if it were *Hakafot* on Simḥat Torah [dancing with a Torah scroll], because I was holding an identity card for the State of Israel in my hand! There was no limit to my happiness and joy. A poll worker brought the ballot box and the chairman of the polling station called to me, quoting from the Torah, 'You shall respect the elderly' (Lev. 19:32), and added that since I was the oldest person present, I would be the first to vote.

"Trembling with reverence and awe, I handed my identity card to the chairman. He read my name from the identity card and his assistant registered it and handed me ballot number one. He also handed me an envelope and I went into a room where the paper slips of all the parties were laid out. With a trembling hand and a feeling of holiness, I took a paper slip from the Religious Union party and placed it in the envelope I had received from the chairman. Then I went back out and showed everyone in the polling station that I had only one envelope. Then came the most sacred moment of my life, which neither my father nor my grandfather had the privilege to experience. Only I, in my time, in my life, was privileged to experience this pure and holy moment.

Blessed am I and blessed is my portion. I put the envelope in the ballot box. I shook hands with the chairman and all the other polling station officials and left the room. I waited in the hall for my wife, because she was second, and after her, my brother, number three, and after him, my brother-in-law, Netanel Saldovin, number four. At 06:28, we returned home and I went to pray. It was a day of great celebration."

And you shall find beauty in their faces

"During Yom HaShoah, Yom HaZikaron, and Yom HaAtzma'ut," writes illustrator Naama Lahav, "everyone looks for old people to talk to. Yes, old people. For schools, for radio and television interviews, for conferences and public gatherings. Someone who escaped from Treblinka, someone who guarded at night in the orchards of a kibbutz, someone who made aliya as a ten-year-old girl under impossible circumstances. We sit in our living rooms or in our cars or with our cell phones in hand and listen openmouthed to unbelievable stories. We look at these people with wonder – how did they endure all of this? Such incredible lives, such unimaginable strength, how much we can learn from them. I think it is to these people that the Torah referred in *parashat Kedoshim* when it says: '*Vehadarta penei zaken*,' 'You shall find beauty in the face of the elderly' (Lev. 19:32).

"We have been taught this mitzva since kindergarten, to the point where we have perhaps forgotten the meaning of the words. It does not mean 'to worry about your elders,' or 'to have mercy upon your elders,' or 'to give your seat on the bus to your elders.' It literally means, 'You shall find beauty in the faces of your elders.' Look at the majestic beauty in those faces, not only on special days, but throughout the year. Make sure to honor, uplift, and glorify the elders in our society. Give respect to every year they have lived and every wrinkle they display."

What unites us?

Between the barbecues and the annual torch lighting ceremony, the World Bible Quiz has also become one of the symbols of Yom HaAtzma'ut (Israel Independence Day). Excited teenagers from around the world take to the stage to be tested on their knowledge of the Bible. When Yuli Edelstein presided as Speaker of the Knesset, he was chairman of the panel of judges for the quiz. One year, he gave the following speech, in which he shared his experiences as a prisoner of Zion (someone incarcerated for pro-Zionist activity) in Soviet Russia:

"I look at you, the contestants. You have come from the United States, Panama, Mexico, Belarus, South Africa.... I look at you, and soon translators will come up here to translate the questions since you do not even share a common language. So what unites you?

"I was once a prisoner of Zion. I was in the Soviet Union, a country that no longer exists, thank God. I taught Hebrew and Judaism. I did not know as much as you, but I knew a little, and that was enough to teach other Jews underground. This did not end well. They put me in prison, and afterward, in a forced labor camp. I was completely cut off, with no way of knowing anything happening outside, beyond the barbed wire, at the end of the world in Siberia.

"One day, we returned from hard labor in the forest after eleven hours in the freezing cold. I crossed through the camp with a line of prisoners, and the officer in charge of prisoner discipline – someone you do not want to mess with – called me out. I went over to him, and he said, 'Just so you know, the safe in my room is full of letters for you from around the world.' Then, with a sadistic smile he continued, 'According to the law, you are not allowed to receive letters from abroad, and you will never see a single letter.' No one could be happier than I was in that moment.

He did not know it, but because of him I suddenly knew that Jews from all over the world were writing to me. This sadist was right. I never did see a single letter, but afterward, I met many people who told me, 'We wrote you letters.' People from countries all over the world, including the countries you have come from. Men and women, young and old, housewives and professors, rabbis and those who did not even know *alef-bet*. People from all walks of life who had nothing in common, but were nevertheless truly united. They knew there was a Jew whom they had never met, and perhaps would never meet, who needed them to fight for his freedom.

"We do not need fake unity, but authentic unity, and you already have it – unity in the most authentic common denominator that we have: the 'book of books,' the Bible. One winner will be announced here today, but that's not important. All of you have already won, because you studied well. I ask of you on Yom HaAtzma'ut, take our shared heritage, the 'book of books,' everywhere and spread its message. When we know the Bible and really internalize it, we will achieve real unity."

Despite the difficulties

Miriam Peretz has every reason to be bitter. She could complain about her childhood in a transit camp, show anger at the fate of her two sons who fell in action while serving in the IDF, weep over the passing of her husband. But her attitude is different. In one of my interviews with her on Yom HaAtzma'ut, I caught a glimpse of her perspective on life:

"We made aliya when I was ten years old. In Morocco, I never went to school. Here in the transit camp, I experienced deprivation that could have made me bitter my entire life. But during my lectures, I turn the tragedy of my absorption in this country into comedy. My father would come to a parents' meetings in his *galabiah* (tunic), and did not understand a word. When they said they were placing me in a vocational stream, as opposed to the academic stream, he thought this was a good idea since I would learn a profession. But I decided at an early age to give thanks for everything I was given, and not to focus on the disparity and difficulties.

"After our marriage, my husband Eliezer and I moved to the community of Ofira at the tip of the Sinai Peninsula near Sharm el-Sheikh. Our sons Uriel and Eliraz were born there. We were the only Orthodox family there, and my husband tried to expand the *minyan* (prayer service). He even tried to get Natan Zahavi (an actor and producer), who was walking on the beach in a bathing suit, to join a *minyan*!

"When the residents of the Yamit region were evacuated in 1982, it was difficult for us, but I made a decision then and there that I would never say to my children, 'The country is gone.' I heard these horrible words after the murder of Rabin, but I knew that my message would never be one of breakdown or failure.

"This mindset helped me with the death of Uriel, and even more so after the death of Eliraz. Choose life with every ounce of strength. In the book of Job, we find the expression, 'Let me speak and I will find relief' (Job 32:20). When I suffered the afflictions of Job, I decided that I would talk and talk, in order to find relief. My husband, of blessed memory, did not speak. He kept everything inside. He held back and repressed everything after Uriel was killed. He surrounded himself with photos of Uriel, and at night I would hear him sigh, 'I would have died in your place' (II Sam. 19:1). After several years, he became ill and passed away. I am the opposite. I continue to speak and tell my story, a story that is really the story of an entire people. 'And you shall tell your son' is not just a dictum for Passover; it is a vital message for the entire year, providing us with strength and giving meaning to our lives."

For the glory of the State of Israel

"For the glory of the State of Israel" – these are the words spoken by each of the twelve honorees after a short speech and before lighting a torch in the annual ceremony held on Mount Herzl on Yom HaAtzma'ut.

Perhaps we need to ask the State of Israel on her birthday the standard birthday question: "What do you want to be when you grow up?" After its inception and development, following the wondrous, physical building of the state, what is her direction, her aspirations, and her goals? The Torah portion of *Kedoshim* (Lev. 19:1–20:27) is always read during this time of year, and it seems to me that part of the answer to these questions can be found there. We may know the passages by heart, but in the month of Iyar they can be reread and understood as the foundation for the revival of Jewish communal life in our homeland. Here are some examples:

> You shall be holy because I, the Lord your God, am holy.
>
> You shall stand before the aged and give honor to the elderly.
>
> Revere your mother and father, and keep My Sabbaths.
>
> You shall not steal. You shall not deceive. You shall not lie to each other.
>
> You shall not oppress your fellow and you shall not rob him. The hired worker's wage shall not remain with you overnight until morning.
>
> You shall not curse the deaf, and you shall not put a stumbling block before the blind.
>
> You shall commit no injustice in judgment. You shall not favor a poor person or give more respect to a great person. You shall judge your fellow with righteousness.
>
> You shall not gossip among your people; you shall not stand idly by the shedding of your fellow's blood.

You shall not hate your brother in your heart.

You shall love your neighbor as yourself... I am the Lord.

The above sounds like an excellent code by which to live for the glory of the State of Israel.

PESAḤ SHENI (SECOND PASSOVER)
It is always possible to make amends

Pesaḥ Sheni falls on the fourteenth of Iyar, one month after Passover. In the book of Numbers, we are told about a group of people who were impure and therefore unable to offer the Passover sacrifice at the proper time. They approached Moses and, in anguish, asked him: "Why should we be deprived?" (Num. 9:7). To answer this question, Moses turned to God, and is told that another date will be set aside, a "second Passover" for people to bring the sacrifice. Whoever was impure or far away on Passover would be able to bring the offering one month later.

Today there is a custom to eat matza on *Pesaḥ Sheni* (although it is still permitted to eat bread as well), but the day serves mainly to remind us that it is okay to give a second opportunity to whoever missed out the first time. As the Lubavitcher Rebbe wrote about this day: "The idea of *Pesaḥ Sheni* is that nothing is ever lost; it is always possible to make amends."

There were those who were indeed forced to observe *Pesaḥ Sheni* in modern times. On the twenty-eighth of Nisan 5705 (1945), with the end of the Second World War, the Buchenwald concentration camp in Germany was liberated. On the fourteenth of Nisan, the Jews in the camp were still enslaved and were not able to celebrate the Passover holiday on its designated date. After the liberation, one month later on the fourteenth of Iyar, they emotionally celebrated it as *Pesaḥ Sheni*.

LAG BAOMER

What happened on Lag BaOmer?

Lag BaOmer, which occurs on the eighteenth of Iyar, is the thirty-third day of counting the Omer. What do we celebrate and why?

1. On the first thirty-two days of counting the Omer, we observe several mourning customs. For example, we do not get married or have a haircut as we mourn for the 24,000 students of Rabbi Akiva who died from a plague during this period. Our Sages say this occurred because the students did not show respect for each other. On Lag BaOmer, the plague ended.

2. After the tremendous loss of Torah scholars, there was a concern over the continuation of Torah study. Some explain that it was on this day that Rabbi Akiva began to teach a new generation of students, among them Rabbi Shimon Bar Yohai. These students ensured the spread of Torah learning among the people. This date thus became a day of celebration and is marked by the cessation of the customs of mourning.

3. Rabbi Shimon Bar Yohai passed away on Lag BaOmer. He was one of the greatest *Tanna'im* (sages who compiled the Mishna during the first two centuries of the Common Era), as well as a symbol of the hidden Torah and the Kabbala. Each year, half a million people go to his grave in Meron, where a gigantic bonfire is lit with much joy and dancing. It is customary to study the Zohar on this day, as well as celebrate with bonfires and sing special liturgical songs.

4. Many families share the custom of waiting until their sons reach the age of three to cut their hair for the first time, and many will wait until Lag BaOmer to do so. Some come to

Meron for the ceremonial haircut, and others will do so by the graves of other *tzaddikim* (righteous people). The idea is that the education of a child, who is ready to start learning Torah at the age of three, should begin with a connection to a *tzaddik*.

5. In the year 2021 (5781), a tragedy occurred in Meron during the course of the Lag BaOmer celebrations. In the worst civil disaster in Israel's history, forty-five people lost their lives because of conditions of extreme overcrowding. Throughout Israel, a national day of mourning was declared. An official committee of enquiry was established in order to investigate the causes of the disaster, and to change the guidelines for future Lag BaOmer festivities.

Rabbi Shimon's secret

When I was little, I remember being asked a philosophical question: "If a tree falls in the forest and no one hears it, does it make a sound?" It seems to me that today we need to ask a new question: "If two teenage girls go to the mall and don't post a selfie, did they really go?" We are living in an age when appearances are everything. If you did not publicize something that you did on social media, it is almost as if it did not happen. We are judged by how we look, our grades, our salary, and the number of "followers" we have. Privacy is dead, and everyone knows everything – the moment it happens.

Lag BaOmer is a day that celebrates the secret Torah. This is the day that Rabbi Shimon Bar Yoḥai, the rabbi of the Kabbala, of what is hidden, passed away. Why is he so beloved? There were many Torah scholars during his time, so what is Rabbi Shimon Bar Yoḥai's secret? The secret is that he revealed the existence of secrets. There are hidden, internal mysteries. The Torah is deserving of a deep connection. The Torah demands hard work and dedication in order to discover her secrets. This is true not only in relation to Torah, but to everything in life: our spouse, children, friends, and indeed every person we meet. We must not be satisfied connecting on just a superficial level. Appearances can be deceiving. Inside, there is a soul. Infinite worlds are hidden beneath the superficial shell that we see at first glance.

Giving of the hidden Torah

What lessons from Rabbi Shimon Bar Yoḥai can we learn for our daily lives? The Slonimer Rebbe (Rabbi Sholom Noach Berezovsky) writes the following in his book *Netivot Shalom*:

"It is fitting to clarify the holiness of this day. It is said that on this day we honor the giving of the hidden Torah. Just as the revealed Torah was accepted by Moses on Mount Sinai, the hidden Torah was revealed by Rabbi Shimon Bar Yoḥai. Every year on this day, the light of the hidden, inner Torah emanates throughout the universe and every person can absorb its holiness and be illuminated by it.

"And so, what is the message of Rabbi Shimon? Nullification of being. This is what he did during his thirteen years in the cave (when he hid from the Romans who sought to kill him). Self-nullification is the root of happiness. As long as a person is fully self-absorbed, with his entire world revolving around him, it is impossible for him to be happy because there will always be matters concerning his body and soul that will not be to his liking and cause him distress, thus excluding the possibility for happiness. Only when a person is released from self-absorption and selfishness and worldly concerns, released from all forms of jealousy, lust, anger, and their like, can he be happy with himself, with others, and with the Holy One, blessed be He. As the Rebbe from Karlin said: 'How full of light and sweetness the world is – for whomever is not immersed in it.'"

From the teachings of Rabbi Shimon

On the anniversary of the passing of a *tzaddik*, it is customary to learn from his teachings. Here are two thoughts from Rabbi Shimon Bar Yoḥai:

"It is better for a person to throw himself into a fiery furnace than to embarrass his fellow in public" (Berakhot 43b) – to such an extent was Rabbi Shimon Bar Yoḥai concerned with the honor of others. The one in whose honor we light our bonfires is telling us that it is preferable to be consumed by fire than to insult or shame someone else in public.

"Strife within the home is worse than the war between Gog and Magog." Relationships within the home are the foundation of society. A war between Gog and Magog sounds like a deadly event, but according to Rabbi Shimon, strife between children and parents or between siblings can have even more catastrophic consequences. The culture of the home, the language spoken, and the honor given to each family member are of even greater importance.

The *shiva* for the Meron tragedy

During the days of the *shiva* for the Meron tragedy, in forty-five houses of mourning throughout Israel, thousands (!) of people visited daily to offer comfort, but also to encounter and speak for the first time. "It's embarrassing that it took a tragedy like this for me to enter the house of a *ḥaredi* family for the first time," someone said to one of the mourning families. They responded, "We also feel bad that it took a tragedy like this for us to host non-religious people in our house for the first time."

During *shiva*, I arrived at the Zakbachs' home in Bnei Brak. Menaḥem, age twenty-four, was survived by his wife Racheli, seven months pregnant, and their young daughter. Racheli showed me that in his memory, they had printed the text of the blessing after the meal, in a pocket-size format. "We printed three thousand copies, and they are already all gone. Who would have imagined that so many people would have come?"

In the family's kitchen, there is no space to move. There are packages upon packages sent by companies, but mostly by individuals, who keep delivering games, clothes, and food. "Even if they're things that we don't need, it means so much to us," the family members said.

A young man came to visit and shared that he had not turned on the television or gone online for all of Shabbat. "I knew that I would see their pictures there, and I knew that they would not have wanted that." He told the Zakbachs that he had felt a particular connection to their son's face, and felt a need to come visit them.

It wasn't easy to sit because more and more people were constantly coming in and standing in the doorway. "Please stand," one of the relatives who had taken charge of matters would say now and again to everyone sitting next to Racheli. "Make room for *Am Yisrael*."

How do you recover from a tragedy?

I had a Zoom conversation with Rabbanit Chana Henkin before an audience of over three hundred Canadians. The event had been planned long before the tragedy in Meron, but in the end it occurred during the *shiva*. Here are some of the things that she said over the course of the evening:

- "We talk a lot about Rabbi Shimon Bar Yoḥai. I want to speak about Rabbi Akiva, his teacher. Rabbi Akiva lost 24,000 students. All of his students died. What did he do? He started again, with only five students. Rabbi Shimon Bar Yoḥai was one of these five. We do not lose hope. Rabbi Akiva teaches us to rise up from every situation, every mourning, every loss."

- "After my son, Rav Eitam, was killed in a terror attack along with his wife Naama, I told my students that no one had ever promised me that God was an ATM. You don't press buttons and get what you want. You do need to always look at the gifts that you are left with. In our case: Rav Eitam and Naama's four children, who survived the attack."

- "There is something else that gives me strength. A rabbi once asked his students, 'How many books are there in the Tanakh?' They all immediately answered, 'Twenty-four.' 'Wrong,' the rabbi said. The class insisted, and so the rabbi explained: 'You are right, of course, but in actuality, there are twenty-five. At this very moment, God continues to write the story of the Jewish people and to fulfill His prophecies. We are the heroes of the twenty-fifth book of Tanakh. Everything that happens to us is part of a great story, which started with Bereshit and continues to this day.' This also gives me strength."

TWENTY-EIGHTH OF IYAR:
YOM YERUSHALAYIM (JERUSALEM DAY)
What are we celebrating on Yom Yerushalayim?

On the twenty-eighth of Iyar 5727 (1967), during the Six-Day War, Jerusalem was reunited under Israeli sovereignty. Israeli paratroopers defeated Jordan's Arab Legion and with great emotion, reached the Western Wall. As the years go by, it is perhaps worthwhile to remind ourselves why Yom Yerushalayim is so special:

1. Firstly, we are celebrating not only the liberation of Jerusalem, but also the rescue of Tel Aviv. Whoever was here during the long wait leading up to the Six-Day War will tell you that the very existence of the young Israeli state was in danger. Our nineteen-year-old state was not only saved, but

it grew many times in size, almost returning to the borders of the biblical Land of Israel.

2. It was the fulfillment of a dream. A new immigrant from Ethiopia told me years ago that, in her childhood, each time she and her siblings saw a stork flying over Addis Ababa, they would cry out: "Stork, stork, how is Jerusalem?" When Natan Sharansky and his friends were accused of treason against "mother Russia," they were asked by the court to summarize their case. Sharansky spoke these words: "To this court I have nothing to say, but to the people of Israel and to my wife, I say: Next year in Jerusalem." We are living a two-thousand-year-old prophecy that is now being fulfilled.

3. Most important of all: We celebrate today because of the greatness of the challenge before us. Because of the magnificent opportunity that we received only now, in this generation. We won the lottery, but what will we do with our winnings? Our mission is to transform all of this energy, all the vows and longings and prayers of our people for thousands of years, into a higher purpose. To connect the Jerusalem above with the Jerusalem below, that this city will herald the development of an alternative culture for the entire world. We are on the road to this goal. Our grandfathers' grandfathers could not have imagined that they would merit to pay property taxes in Jerusalem, to get stuck there in traffic jams, or to quarrel over the character of the Holy City. But we have been given that privilege.

Prophecies in the headlines

It is the eighteenth of Iyar, the date of the liberation of the Old City. In order to understand an important event, sometimes it is best to go back for a moment to see what the archives have to say.

The day following the unification of Jerusalem, the newspaper *Haaretz* quoted the prophet Isaiah in giant letters on the front page: "Shout and praise, dwellers of Zion" (Is. 12:6). The editorial of the day read as follows: "There are no words to express the stirring emotions in our hearts at this hour. The Old City of Jerusalem is ours. Its gates are open and the Western Wall will no longer stand silent and deserted. The glory of the past is no longer to be viewed from afar, but from now on will be a part of the new state, and will shine its light on the building of a Jewish society that is a link in the long chain of our nation's history in our land. The entire nation of Israel, here and in the Diaspora, applauds the IDF which has restored the splendor of bygone days."

These moving words are subdued in comparison to the following report from *Haaretz*'s field correspondent: "Whoever saw Jerusalem rejoicing yesterday could perhaps imagine the rejoicing in ancient Jerusalem at the time of the three pilgrimage festivals. In the stirring emotions of the moment, the concept of the Holy Temple suddenly became more tangible. 'Now it will be possible to build the Holy Temple.' This was a statement that came spontaneously from the heart, yet people were also saying it yesterday in all seriousness. A university professor and a physician said it. A high school student said it. Many people were saying it, and not necessarily the religious. Whoever did not see the jubilation in Jerusalem yesterday has never seen jubilation in his life."

Hannah Semer, editor of the newspaper *Davar*, wrote the following the day after the paratroopers reached the Kotel (Western Wall): "A Redeemer has come to Zion. For two thousand years, eighty generations, Jews have turned to the East – in morning, afternoon, and evening prayers. Two thousand years did not blur our national memory; a Jew was born with it just like he was born with all 248 parts of his body. All the biblical verses are resurrected before our eyes."

The above reports comprise a short lesson about the press in those days, about perspective, and about Jerusalem.

We were as dreamers

What follows is one of the most emotional testimonies, in my eyes, of the liberation of the Kotel, courtesy of Rabbi She'ar Yashuv Cohen, who was the Ashkenazi Chief Rabbi of Haifa at the time:

"Several days after the victory, on the first Shavuot holiday following the liberation of the Old City, it was my good fortune to walk to the Kotel among the masses who were accompanying Rabbi Aryeh Levin, the unforgettable *tzaddik* of Jerusalem, who came joyfully toward me and hugged me warmly. We walked together silently, deep in thought. And then he said to me, almost in a whisper, the following words: 'All my life I did not understand the meaning of the verse, "When Hashem returns those in exile to Zion, we will have been like dreamers" (Ps. 125:1). Now I understand.' I asked him, 'What does the good rabbi understand?' He said, 'A dream is like this: A person witnesses in one moment events that have occurred over a long period of time. Sometimes, it's possible to see in a dream something that would take years to occur naturally, but now you see it happening all at once, and in an instant the whole picture becomes clear. An entire epoch, a long history, an experience of generations passes in front of your eyes in a brief moment. In a dream it is possible, in a few seconds, to see the past, the present, and the future. This is what is happening to us now, here. We are entering the Old City, walking to the Kotel, and we are like dreamers. At this very moment we are connected to the thousands and tens of thousands who prayed and looked forward to this moment for generations. And we are living it now. In a flash, we see everyone who was in the Diaspora, in the Holocaust, in the underground, in the wars. Everyone who ever prayed, waited, hoped. And now that time has arrived. Thousands of years culminate in this single moment. We are like dreamers.'"

The heart of our hearts

The late Elie Wiesel, a Nobel Prize-winning author and Holocaust survivor, once published a giant advertisement in the American press. It was during the days of the Obama administration, and Wiesel sought to end the pressure on Israel regarding Jerusalem. He explained the significance of the city in these words:

"For me as a Jew, Jerusalem is above politics. It is mentioned more than six hundred times in the Bible, and not even once in the Koran. Throughout Jewish history, there has been no prayer more moving than that which expresses a longing to return to Jerusalem. It's much more than a city. It connects one Jew to another in a way that will always be difficult to explain. When a Jew visits Jerusalem for the first time, it's not the first time – he's returning home. I once heard in the name of Rabbi Nachman of Breslov, a great hasidic leader, that everything in the world has a heart, and even the heart has a heart. Jerusalem is the heart of our hearts."

Stay in low gear

The following story about Jerusalem conveys the feelings it can awaken within us.

Professor Nechama Leibowitz, the eminent Bible teacher and recipient of the Israel Prize, made aliya to Israel in the days of the British Mandate. On her way to Jerusalem for the first time, the twenty-five-year-old immigrant experienced the many ascents and descents with which we are all familiar. On one of the curves in the road, she and her husband saw a sign that read: "Remain in low gear." They only knew biblical Hebrew, not spoken Hebrew, and Nechama understood this as spiritual instruction for whoever is "going up" to Jerusalem: stay in low gear – in other words, keep yourself small; stay humble and unpretentious as you approach the gates of the city. "How beautiful," she said to her husband. "In the Land of Israel, there are road signs that remind those going up to the holy city to enter with humility, in the proper spirit."

Sivan

ENTERING THE MONTH OF SIVAN
We and our descendants

A wise man once told me that he had many professional ambitions, but above all, he wanted to be a better father, a better husband, a better son, a better brother, and a better grandson. At the end of life, a person can look back on his many achievements, but life's work is not only the degrees he earned or his profession; it is primarily about family.

As the new month of Sivan begins, just days before Shavuot, the festival of the giving of the Torah, it is customary to pray in this vein. Over four hundred years ago, the Shelah HaKadosh (Rabbi Yeshayahu HaLevi Horowitz) instituted a tradition to pray for our children's education. Parents have repeated his prayer throughout the generations, and still do so today. Here is a taste:

"Let us and our descendants and the descendants of all of Your people Israel know Your name and study Your Torah.... And give them health and honor and strength, and give them high stature and beauty and grace and kindness, and let there be love and brotherhood and peace between them, and may they worship You with love and awe.... Grant them nothing but peace and

truth and let them be good and honest in the eyes of God and in
the eyes of man."

SHAVUOT
What is the meaning of Shavuot?

1. The festival of Shavuot is celebrated on the sixth of Sivan.
   It is called by this name since the seven weeks (*"shavuot"* is
   Hebrew for "weeks") of counting the Omer that began on
   Passover end on this day.

2. Shavuot is the festival of the giving of the Torah, and
   during the morning prayer service in synagogue we read
   the passages which describe receiving the Ten Commandments on Mount Sinai. We study Torah all night
   long through *Tikkun Leil Shavuot* (which refers both to
   the study session and to the text traditionally used for it,
   although other texts are commonly studied, or in many
   communities, a series of seminars may be given on a
   relevant topic). According to tradition, on the morning
   of the giving of the Torah, the nation of Israel was still
   fast asleep. In order to atone for this error, the children of
   Israel undertook not to sleep on this night but to stay up
   and study in order to reach the morning awake and ready
   to receive the Torah.

3. Shavuot is also called *Ḥag HaKatzir* (the Harvest Festival)
   or *Ḥag HaBikkurim* (Festival of the First Fruits). When the
   Holy Temple stood, the first offering from the new wheat
   crop, known as the *Shtei HaLeḥem* (the two loaves), was
   brought, celebrating the wheat harvest and the ripening
   of the first fruits, and ushering in a season that would last
   until Sukkot.

4. On the festival of Shavuot, it is customary to read *Megillat Rut* (the Book of Ruth). Ruth converted to Judaism and joined the nation of Israel, ultimately meriting to be the ancestress of King David. The story is a reminder that every person, regardless of origin, can choose to accept the Torah.

5. Some have the custom of adorning their homes and synagogue with plants, a reminder of Mount Sinai that blossomed with plants in honor of the giving of the Torah. There are also those who include honey and milk in their menus to symbolize the Torah, which is said to be like "honey and milk under your tongue" (Song. 4:11).

The Statue of Liberty is not enough

Although we gained our freedom upon leaving Egypt, freedom is not enough. We must fill freedom with content. The renowned psychiatrist Viktor Frankl, a Holocaust survivor and author of *Man's Search for Meaning*, wrote that the United States needs not only a Statue of Liberty, but also a Statue of Responsibility. The values of freedom are important, but once we are no longer enslaved – what next? What is our identity? What are the new values that obligate us? We do not need only rights, but also obligations. In the context of Frankl's thought, perhaps we can say that if Passover is the festival of freedom, then Shavuot is the festival of responsibility.

Our chapter in the book

Rabbi Jonathan Sacks, of blessed memory, was the Chief Rabbi of Great Britain, a professor in several universities, a member of the British House of Lords, and a lecturer and highly sought-after speaker throughout the world. He had a broad understanding of many issues and made a lasting impression with his wealth of knowledge, but he had a particularly strong sense of urgency regarding one matter – the struggle against assimilation and what needed to be done to ensure Jewish continuity.

Rabbi Sacks met numerous young Jews from throughout the world who, according to statistics, should have disappeared from Jewish life. He repeated the following story over and over again in order to connect these young Jews to the Torah, in the hope that they would add another link in the chain of Jewish continuity that began at Mount Sinai:

Imagine a huge library full of books. Room after room filled with the world's greatest literature. You can take any book that you wish, either read it a little or immerse yourself fully, and then return it to the shelf and choose another. How fun. There would be no limit to the possibilities in front of you. Indeed, Western culture does offer us such wealth, Rabbi Sacks explained, but Judaism presents us with a different story:

Imagine that while searching in that library you come across a single book, different from the rest, which captures your attention because your family name appears on the cover. You open it with curiosity, and slowly realize that this is an extraordinary book – each generation that preceded you tells its story for the sake of the next generation and so on, generation after generation until your own. Anyone born into this family will be able to learn where he came from, what happened to his predecessors, for what purpose they lived, and why. As you finish reading, you come to a blank page, except for the title. The title bears your name.

This is not just another book. This is your story. Each of us is here thanks to a long chain of people who participated in the journey toward a particular destination. The journey is not over; it is waiting for us to move onward. Will we write our own chapter in the book?

Only one Yosef

A famous saying associated with the holiday of Shavuot is found in the tractate of Pesaḥim in the Talmud. Every year on Shavuot, Rabbi Yosef would hold a special feast and declare: "If it were not for what happened on this day, how many Yosefs would there be in the market?" (Pesaḥim 68b). In other words, if it were not for the giving of the Torah, I, Yosef, would be like everyone else you find in the market and the streets. In the merit of the Torah, I am not.

Rabbi Omer Levi, a Chabad emissary in Ramat Gan, offers a wonderful commentary on this declaration: Rabbi Yosef does not mean to offend whoever is in the market or in the world at large. That is not his intention. He is talking about himself. He is saying that if it wasn't for this day, he would be many Yosefs. Indeed, all of us wear many different masks. There is the mask we wear at home, the one we wear in the market, the one we wear at work, and the one we wear on Facebook. If it not for this day, Rabbi Yosef is saying, I would be confused, running between temptations and a multitude of everyday matters, pretending to be this or that, not focused, not authentic. If not for this day when we received the Torah, there would be many versions of me, like a chameleon that continually changes its colors in response to its surroundings. According to this interpretation, in the face of perpetual distraction, the Torah provides stability and focus, and connects all the different areas of life. Instead of there being many Yosefs agitating inside us and confusing us, there is just one Yosef.

Do you want the gift?

We hear a lot about the significance of Torah in different contexts in our public dialogue, but have we ever heard it described as a gift? Here is a thought offered by Rabbi Shimshon Dovid Pincus about the festival of Shavuot, when we celebrate the giving of the Torah:

"If someone wears a beautiful watch on his wrist, he is often asked where he bought it. But if we see a poor person holding a diamond worth five million dollars, we will not ask, 'Where did you buy it?' but rather, 'Who gave you that gift?' because we wouldn't imagine that he bought it himself. The holy Torah is a most valuable gift. As long we study it and do good deeds – it will carry on giving. All that is required of us is one thing: desire, to want and appreciate the gift. Our obligation on Shavuot is nothing more than to want the Torah, to see its importance. A person will agree to give his friend a precious diamond only if he knows that his friend will appreciate and look after it. He will not give the diamond to someone who will play with it in the sand.

"Every year, on the eve of Shavuot, the Holy One, blessed be He travels the world and asks each one of us: Are you interested in receiving the Torah? Do you want it? And we answer: Yes. '*Naaseh venishma*' (We will do [what it instructs] and we will understand [later]). Despite our limitations, if we really want it, we will be gifted an abundance of Torah on Shavuot."

It's not Acamol (paracetamol)

In a generation where many young people want to take the quick and easy route, Rabbi Yehuda Amital, the head of Yeshivat Har Tzion, demanded from his students thoroughness, depth, and diligence. In this context, he explained why we need to relate much more seriously to our Torah, especially today:

"I have nothing against Acamol (paracetamol), but whoever thinks we can cure the ailments of a generation with popular songs, playing on the emotions, is mistaken. It is just like taking Acamol. Any enthusiasm is temporary, and you need something new each time. There is nothing tangible there that will stay with you when it is over. Torah study is an asset that always remains with you, even if you should put it aside. It continues to be relevant and is not only for quick relief like Acamol. We must return to the path of studying hard, toiling for knowledge, and completely immersing ourselves in Torah. The brain, our source of intellectual strength, is the human being's most important organ. Can we suffice in our service of Hashem only with our hands and other limbs? Will we take a shofar in our hands and blow into it with our mouth, put on tefillin, eat matza – but neglect to use our brains? Whoever does not occupy himself with learning Torah is lacking something fundamental. Will we use our brains only for our career, for attaining an academic degree, and leave service of Hashem to the rest of our organs and limbs?"

A new kind of unity

We are used to uniting against enemies, but our unity on the holiday of Shavuot is different. Rabbi Shalom Rosner, who made aliya from the United States and is a rabbi in Beit Shemesh, writes that when it comes to terrorism and wars, we excel in solidarity. There are many examples of an external enemy strengthening our sense of solidarity. This is important, but our stature when we stood together at Mount Sinai heralded a revolution. It raised us up to a new level of unity.

At Mount Sinai, we were not fleeing a frightening foe, but came together in joy to receive our new identity. We did not crowd closely together, side by side, because of Pharaoh and the Egyptians, the Nazis and anti-Semites or any other threat, but instead chose to be together to receive the Ten Commandments. We were not defined by a negative experience, but by a positive one – not by what we feared, but by what we wanted to be. We often experience the first type of unity, facing a hostile military force. But on the holiday of Shavuot, it is possible to ascend to the highest level: unity around our common purpose and the gift we received together at Mount Sinai.

Which fingerprints are yours?

Whoever is reading these words has their own fingerprints, different, unique, unmatchable. No two people have the same fingerprints. Rabbi Avraham Yitzchak HaCohen Kook, Israel's first Chief Rabbi, explained that each person's connection to the Torah is equally unique and creates its special light. On the holiday of Shavuot, when we receive the Torah anew, we are likely to think that our part in the story is not so critical. Indeed, there are approximately fourteen million Jews in the world, and many of them are wiser and more righteous than we are, so why are we so important?

Rav Kook writes: "The light that is created from one person's connection to the Torah is different from the light created from another person's connection to the Torah. And so each person expands the Torah when he studies it." In other words, each soul that learns Torah creates a unique connection and gives birth to new light in the world that never was and, otherwise, would never be. We cannot just copy someone else's work, and we cannot be satisfied that others are learning Torah. Each person must create his own special light.

A historic inn

What is the significance of learning Torah? What happens when we learn? Rabbi Yosef Dov Soloveitchik, of blessed memory, who was an eminent leader of American Jewry, explains the following:

"When I sit down to learn, I immediately find myself in the presence of a group of devoted sages, learned in tradition and values. The relationship between us is personal. The Rambam is on my right; Rabbeinu Tam is on my left. Rashi sits at the head of the table and makes clarifications to which Rabbeinu Tam objects. The Rambam makes a ruling and the Raavad challenges it. All of them are in my little room, sitting around my table. They look at me with affection, play with me through *sevara* (logic) and Gemara (Talmud), encouraging and strengthening me. Learning

Torah is not just a didactic exercise. Learning Torah is not just a formal, technical preoccupation that involves exchange of information and inventive thinking. Learning Torah is an unparalleled experience of friendship through many generations, of connection between spirits and unity between souls of different eras. Those who passed on their Torah wisdom and those who receive it are united in the same historic inn."

Throughout the year, and especially on the festival of Shavuot, we are invited to join company in the very same historic inn.

Small acts of kindness

On the holiday of Shavuot, it is customary to read the Book of Ruth. Dr. Yael Ziegler, a college lecturer on the Bible, notes that in the Book of Ruth there are no big headlines, only simple, unacknowledged, everyday acts. Ruth embodies kindness in how she treats her mother-in-law Naomi, but no one has any knowledge of this at the time. Boaz behaves with courtesy and generosity toward Ruth, but no one gives him a prize for doing so. Slowly, slowly, Ruth and Boaz create a new family based on outstanding character traits, trust, and concern for others. A new family tree grows out of these inconspicuous good deeds. From a collection of acts that lack any real drama, a most dramatic event ultimately occurs – King David is born.

The Book of Ruth teaches us to take a deeper look at reality, with more attention devoted to details that appear minor but have eternal significance. Why should anyone care about a foreign girl collecting sheaves of wheat left behind by reapers in a field? Why should we give of ourselves to an old widow? Today we can also ask: Why is it important if we secretly do one more good deed; who cares about one more mitzva or one more smile or helping hand? What difference does it make? The Book of Ruth teaches us that these little acts of kindness are of the greatest importance.

The pleasant path to faith

What gives people their faith? How does someone develop belief in God? I heard the following idea from Mrs. Esther Wein from New York:

There are three figures who discovered faith in God and changed their lives:

Avraham Avinu explored the world, examined the entire creation and, in this manner, arrived at his faith. He was driven by scientific analysis, research, and logic.

Yitro (Jethro), Moses's father-in-law, joined the Jewish people and came to his belief in their God in a different way. Yitro, a pagan priest, looked at history and recognized God's involvement in world events and miracles. He heard about the Exodus from Egypt, the splitting of the Red Sea – and he joined the people of Israel.

On Shavuot, we read the story of Ruth, whose path was entirely different. Ruth joined our nation after meeting a kind and pleasant person, Naomi. Naomi, true to her name (Naomi is cognate with *no'am/na'im*, meaning "pleasant"), was the embodiment of pleasantness. She was an honest woman who was full of kindness and compassion above and beyond her strong faith. Her pleasantness, day in and day out, found favor in the eyes of Ruth, who simply wanted to stay by her side. We can see in the famous words that Ruth says to Naomi that she feels a connection to Naomi, and through it, also to the people and to God: "Wherever you go I will go, and where you stay I will stay. Your people will be my people, and your God my God."

At that time, Naomi was a widow, impoverished and alone, yet despite all this, she was a wonderful, noble person with strong values. This pleasantness attracted Ruth, caused her to join our people, and from her descendants, King David was born."

May we all merit to find such pleasantness in our lives.

Learning for the sake of learning

"All the Torah that millions of Jews throughout the world learn during the festival of Shavuot could be condensed into a single computer file, not too large, to be quickly accessed at any time," writes Rabbi Manny Even Yisrael. "So what's the point of learning the material over and over again? Why do people sit in front of these texts, especially when they receive nothing, no degree or certificate, in return?"

The rabbi's answer is also good advice to all of us on the day after the giving of the Torah:

"The Torah offers us something new: learning for the sake of learning. In a competitive world, this is indeed something exceptional. The Torah is not information; it is our identity. The Torah demands not only the head, but the heart and soul, too. The Torah connects us to ourselves and to the One who gave it. The real challenge comes the day after Shavuot. How do we maintain this connection? At Mount Sinai, after the giving of the Torah, the children of Israel became confused and made a Golden Calf. Today, we need to think how to leverage the festival of Shavuot in a positive way. Day after day, we counted the Omer, but exactly like a couple that excitedly prepared for their wedding day, we could find ourselves the day after the wedding settled into a dull routine. I suggest that we all find a part of the Torah to which we are especially connected that gives us strength and meaning, and commit to learning that particular part of Torah on a regular basis, throughout the year, even on a small scale."

Tamuz

THIRD OF TAMUZ

What did I learn from the Rebbe?

Rabbi Menachem Mendel Schneerson was the leader of the Chabad movement in our generation, established thousands of Chabad houses with emissaries throughout the world, and is considered one of the most influential Jews of all time. I was once asked: What did you learn from the Lubavitcher Rebbe, and what can we continue to learn from him after his passing on the third of Tamuz 5754 (1994)?

My answer is: Jewish pride. In a generation of American Jews who were embarrassed to keep Shabbat, keep kosher, and wear a *kippa*, the Rebbe created a new model of a proud Jew: someone who succeeds within the surrounding culture without forgetting who he is. He once explained it like this: "Abraham did not consider popular opinion in his day, and not only did he educate his family in his new faith, he also publicized it through-out the world. In response, the nations of the world admired him. When we know who we are and respect ourselves, others respect us as well."

The Rebbe also taught us about the relationship between the present and the future. I once heard a precise description of the Lubavitcher Rebbe from Shimon Peres: "The Rebbe saw the future with the same degree of clarity as he saw the present." Most of us are limited in seeing only the present reality around us, and do not really believe in our ability to change it. How important it is for us to see the existing situation (within ourselves, our family, the nation of Israel, and the world as a whole) and to believe, truly believe, that it can change. When we say the words "Next year in Jerusalem" or "May our eyes behold Your return to Zion," we shouldn't just give lip service to them. It is important to believe this is really possible, and to act in practical ways to advance this goal.

We also learn about positive spiritual influence. When I was young, I was suspicious of being "brainwashed by rabbis." I heard about someone who asked the Lubavitcher Rebbe: "If you told your Hasidim to jump off a roof, would they jump?" The Rebbe answered: "This is not the right question, because I would never tell them to jump off a roof. On the contrary, my task is to always lift those around me one *tefaḥ* (8–10 centimeters or 3–4 inches) above the ground." There can be negative spiritual influence, but we must seek out those who will influence us spiritually in a positive way.

Spreading Judaism with technological tools

Appropriate involvement with mass media is the biggest challenge of this generation. It is difficult to make use of the social networks without them using us in return. On the one hand, the Lubavitcher Rebbe warned us against being enslaved to the media – that is, enslavement to the improper values that the media often promotes. On the other hand, he guided us as to how to make use of the newest technologies in order to spread Judaism.

In the 1950s, the Rebbe was criticized when radio programs that were sponsored by Chabad began to air. There were religious Jews who said that radio was an impure means of communication and it should not be utilized by a rebbe. The Rebbe's response was fascinating. He explained that the radio, like every other techno-logical development, is a tool in the world of the Holy One, blessed be He. The Rebbe mentioned the well-known saying that the Baal Shem Tov heard, according to which the Messiah will come when "your wellsprings shall go forth and spread outside." The Rebbe noted that the radio brings the wellsprings of the Torah "outside" to the greatest possible extent: "As long as there are any places where the wellsprings have not yet spread, then our mission to do so has not succeeded, since there is still an 'outside' that has not yet been reached."

The Rebbe had a very special relationship with journalists, and did not regard them solely as impersonal professionals. The Rebbe pleaded in one of his letters "not to be an armchair journal-ist." In other words, not to look at reality as a detached observer and reporter, but rather to experience events and to personally participate in them.

In his many conversations and meetings with media people, the Rebbe explained that words of Torah are an integral part of the daily news. It is our job to see them in the context of every-day events and report them as such. He urged talking about the Torah portion of the week, since it too is part of the news and the headlines, no less important than updates on what is happen-ing in Washington or Tehran. Once, in a 1980 meeting with Moti Eden, who was a reporter and news editor with "Kol Yisrael" at the time, the Rebbe spoke of the relevance of the Torah to every per-son, at every moment in history: "*Shema Yisrael, Hashem Elokeinu, Hashem Eḥad* – this declaration was not only meant for the people who stood at Mount Sinai three thousand years ago, but for every Abraham, Moses, and Solomon living in Tel Aviv, on such and such a street, at such and such a number. Hashem was speaking to them when He said '*Shema Yisrael*.'"

Do not shout, but whisper

In an era when it seems that everybody shouts, here is a short but important story about a different approach:

Rabbi Moshe Feller, the Chabad emissary in Minnesota, was asked to write an article about Judaism for a local newspaper. He tried to explain its great impact on our lives, and wrote that when a person faints and loses consciousness, we are instructed to lean close to his ear and shout his name in order to wake him up. In the same way, when a person is far from Judaism, from his identity, from himself – you need to shout his name, shout that he is a Jew, and he will remember who he is and reawaken (spiritually). Rabbi Feller sent the article to the Lubavitcher Rebbe, who corrected just one word. It was a change that had great significance. He crossed out "shout" and wrote above it "whisper." Not to shout into the other's ear, but to whisper into it.

How do you influence someone? How do you approach someone who is far away? Don't shout at him that he is mistaken; don't roar at him with your beliefs. Rather, whisper. You are about to enter a delicate place – his soul. Don't approach him aggressively; approach him calmly, with care and with love.

More than two decades have passed since we were privileged to hear the Rebbe's whispers, but we are in need of his approach now more than ever.

There is no pension for spiritual work

Every year on the third of Tamuz it seems that the task left for us by the Lubavitcher Rebbe is more relevant than ever: to touch every soul, to change the world, and to understand that every single person is an emissary. Here are three particularly empowering quotes from the book *Ma Shelamadeti MeHaRebbe* by Rabbi Shneur Ashkenazi:

"God created the world such that each person is unique, and no two people can be identical. The reason for this is that each person has a personal role to fulfil that none other can do, and this role is vital to fulfilling the purpose of Creation."

The Rebbe once wrote to someone who was unwell: "There is a well-known hasidic saying: 'Think good and it will be good.' It would seem that we must wait until our health improves before we can rejoice. But we say the opposite: It is better to rejoice in advance, and this in itself will hasten our recovery."

To someone who retired and became a pensioner, he wrote: "Retirement from work is relevant only in material matters, in business and earning a livelihood. It is important to know that there is no retiring from spiritual work and service. This work is a most precious lifetime mission, and indeed it can be increased all the more when retirement comes."

SEVENTEENTH OF TAMUZ
The holiness of a routine

We fast on the Seventeenth of Tamuz to commemorate five events that happened on this day: the Tablets of the Covenant were broken in the desert; the *tamid* (daily) sacrifice at the time of the first Temple was stopped; the walls of Jerusalem were breached by the Romans at the time of the Second Temple; a Torah scroll was burned by Apostomus; and he also placed an idol in the Temple Sanctuary.

The *tamid* sacrifice was performed each morning and evening in the Holy Temple. What is so significant about the permanence of this daily act? There is a fascinating Midrash in which our Sages discuss which verse in the Torah is most important (*Sifra* 4:12). This is expanded upon in the introduction to *Ein Yaakov* (a collection of talmudic aggadot, or tales) as follows: One sage says the most important verse is "*Shema Yisrael*," a second sage says it is "Love your fellow as yourself," and a third says it is "You shall offer one sheep in the morning and another toward evening." Ultimately, this last verse was deemed to be most important. This is surprising! Why is this verse the most important? Most of us are probably not even familiar with it. Well, unlike those verses that contain some form of drama or wow factor, this verse describes the daily *tamid* sacrifice, a routine, doing something every morning and every evening. It is this element of our identity that is probably the most important in relation to ourselves, our children, our spouses, and our nation too. It is the ability to persevere and adhere to our values, finding in them beauty and meaning. This is the source of our strength.

It may seem that the most difficult aspect of our lives is our routine. Preparing food, doing the same work in the office day after day, praying the same prayers. On the Seventeenth of Tamuz we mourn, among other events, the loss of the daily *tamid* sacrifice. It was a quiet, daily devotion without explosions or trumpets or "likes." It was the rock of our existence.

What do we still mourn today?

On the Seventeenth of Tamuz, the walls of Jerusalem were breached. The day was designated as a fast day, and it is the beginning of the mourning period known as "*bein ḥametzarim,*" "between the straits." Rabbi Menachem Brod wrote about why we still mourn today:

"We have returned to our beautiful and blossoming land. We have returned to Jerusalem. So what is there to mourn? The concept of *galut* (exile) is not confined to the question of whether the nation of Israel lives in Morocco, America, or in the Land of Israel. The question is *how* we live. We have made much progress in this generation, but subjugation can exist even when we live in Jerusalem, because the essence of exile is internal, a frame of mind. The very fact that it seems to us that the way things are today is good enough is part and parcel of the mindset of exile. It is human nature to get used to things as they are. Exile brings us to the point where our human potential is channeled in negative, not positive ways – where there is so much violence, corruption, division, and baseless hatred; where the Torah is considered a burden instead of the most natural and pleasant gift; where we forget our true essence and that we have been called to greatness. The days "between the straits" that begin now are a sign, a reminder, an annual opportunity for soul-searching and thinking not only about what we have already achieved, but also what we still have to accomplish."

BETWEEN THE STRAITS
Don't hide the suffering

Between the fast of the Seventeenth of Tamuz and the fast of the Ninth of Av (Tisha B'Av), we are in a state of "between the straits," a phrase taken from the Book of Lamentations (1:3). This period is also known as "the three weeks." During this time, we adopt mourning practices which become more stringent as we approach Tisha B'Av.

"It is not by chance that 'the three weeks' arrive during the summer vacation," explains Rabbanit Yemima Mizrachi. "Indeed, the days 'between the straits' are the days when children learn from their home environment, even though the days that follow could be called 'between the guest houses' as we travel the country on family excursions. But in fact, the most important lessons for the people of Israel are not learned at school. Instead, the 'Divine Ministry of Education' insists that stories about this period should be passed directly from father to son rather than filtered through school.

"When I was young, my father used to sit us all down and tell heartfelt stories about the destruction of the Holy Temple, until my mother begged him to stop. My father's behavior was the opposite of our natural tendency as parents to spare our children from the world's sorrows. Parents naturally protect their children from the hard work, the challenges, the difficult road we traversed so that everything will seem comfortable and easy for them. But life is not easy. Children can become accustomed to abundance and not value what they have. Memories of the past are not just a story, but a slice of reality. Our job is to connect our children – with sensitivity – to the long and burdensome road that we traveled in the past. Perhaps, in this way, they will be more prepared to deal with personal trials. If they know it was difficult in the past, and that for others it is still difficult today, they may cope differently with the challenges they will one day encounter in parenting and marriage. If they hear stories about their ancestors, they will understand that their roots run deep, and then their wings will be broader too. So tell them about Grandma's experience in the Holocaust, about Father losing his job, about poverty, about hard times. This way they will remember from where they came and understand the secret of redemption."

A parallel universe

Where would we be today if not for COVID-19? What would our lives, having changed so much due to the pandemic, be like? Rabbi Hillel Merzbach, a rabbi in the community of Yad Binyamin, suggests we also ask these questions regarding the days "between the straits," and to imagine a parallel universe, a world without the tragedies commemorated at this time of year:

"On the Seventeenth of Tamuz, the sin of the Golden Calf occurred. If we had not sinned on that day, Moses would have come down from Mount Sinai without breaking the Tablets and he would have given them to us with great celebration. The Seventeenth of Tamuz would have been forever known as the date of Simḥat Torah, the day we received the Tablets of the Covenant.

"On Tisha B'Av, the sin of the spies occurred with their negative report of what they found in the Land of Israel. If the spies had returned full of optimism and excitement and inspired the people, this date would have been eternally joyful, celebrating our entry into the Land of Israel with love. We missed opportunities, we messed up, but this is our chance to recall what happened, mourn what we did, and try to rectify our deeds. On the Seventeenth of Tamuz we disrespected the Torah, and on the Ninth of Av we disrespected the Land of Israel. We now have three weeks to repent and correct the events of this period of time."

Av

THE NINE DAYS
Looking pain in the eye

"When Adar begins, we increase our joy" (Taanit 29a) is a well-known saying, but there is another side to the coin: "When Av begins, we decrease our joy." The period of mourning began on the Seventeenth of Tamuz, when we ushered in "the three weeks," also known as "between the straits." However, on the first of Av, our mourning intensifies with the onset of "the nine days." Just as Sukkot is "the time of our rejoicing" and Passover is "the time of our freedom," now is the time of our mourning. Rabbi Erez Moshe Doron, as a Breslov Hasid for whom "it is a great mitzva to always be happy," explains that on Tisha B'Av we must not shy away from seeing the pain and looking it straight in the eye:

"Generally speaking, we look for ways to find solace and distract ourselves from sorrow. But at this time of year, we are called upon to pay attention to the sorrow in our imperfect reality. We do not try to escape it or do everything possible in order not to feel the pain, as has become customary in Western culture. Yes, there is evil in the world, and bitterness. Yet we are not asking just for consolation or temporary relief but for complete redemption, a transformation of reality, perfection itself. At this time of year we are called upon to fight for the world, to fight for the nation of Israel, which is supposed to be different. It is not by chance that our sources say that when we ascend to the heavenly court on high, we will be asked, 'Did you wait expectantly for salvation?' In other words: Did you really want change? Did you believe that improvement was truly possible? We tend to ask for the maximum when it comes to money and material possessions, but at this time of year we seek the maximum when it comes to the spiritual aspects of life – peace of mind, Torah, holiness, and inner happiness."

Just listening is enough

Aaron the High Priest passed away on Rosh Ḥodesh Av (Rosh Ḥodesh is the first day of the new month). The exact date of his death is the only one mentioned in the entire bible. Rabbi Zevik Harel, an educator from the community of Bnei Dekalim, writes about our mission based on Aaron's legacy:

"Aaron the High Priest, who passed away on Rosh Ḥodesh Av, is associated with love, listening, and caring. From the very beginning, he regarded his brother Moses's position as leader not only in a positive light, but with genuine happiness, and ultimately became a symbol of peace for the people of Israel. Hillel the Elder said: 'Be like the disciples of Aaron who love peace and pursue peace, love all of God's creation, and come close to the Torah' (Mishna Avot 1:12). Our Sages say that Aaron would listen carefully to every person in order to understand each one's pain. He would find the beauty in every individual and succeed in strengthening and encouraging that person in the process.

"We live in a world based on productivity, with numerous courses offered on effective public speaking, time management, branding, and marketing, but no courses are offered on listening. Listening is considered dull and boring, yet to truly hear someone is never passive; it demands active engagement. To listen is to go outside myself, to give all of what I am to another and to understand the place that person is coming from. In such moments, the Holy Temple begins to be rebuilt.

"Every time the famous Jerusalem *tzaddik*, Rabbi Aryeh Levin, visited a prison or a hospital, those he visited were left spiritually stirred and uplifted by his presence. Once, a member of the staff approached him and said: 'Reb Aryeh, I must ask you something. How is it that everyone is so happy after your visit? What do you say to them?' Reb Aryeh answered, 'I don't say anything to them. I just try to listen.'"

Important words to start the day

The Ari HaKadosh, Rabbi Yitzchak Ben Shlomo Luria, passed away on the fifth of Av 5032 (1572). He studied and elucidated Kabbala, but how can we, inferior in our understanding, even begin to approach Kabbala? The Ari learned and taught about exile and redemption, impurity and holiness, this world and the next. He taught his students about the anguish of the *Shekhina* (Divine Presence), rectification of the soul, and the ten *Sefirot*, the attributes through which God manifests Himself. He also left writings containing special *kavanot* (intentions to keep in mind during prayers) and liturgical poems in Aramaic with hidden meanings.

But there is one clear and simple message that everyone can understand, especially as Tisha B'Av approaches. He asked that we recite the following sentence prior to morning prayers: "I hereby take upon myself to fulfill the mitzva of 'Love your fellow as yourself.'" He explained that the mitzva of loving every Jew is the gateway through which we must pass before we begin to pray. Whoever loves the Creator must first love His creations. And to do this, we do not need to be kabbalists.

SHABBAT ḤAZON (SABBATH OF VISION)
What is your vision?

The Shabbat before Tisha B'Av is called *Shabbat Ḥazon*, named in recognition of the *haftara* that we read, which opens with this verse: "The vision of Isaiah the son of Amotz, which he saw concerning [the geographical region of] Yehuda and Jerusalem" (Is. 1:1). This *haftara* describes the difficult spiritual condition of the people in the days of the First Temple: "Israel does not know; My people do not understand.... Your princes are rebellious and companions of thieves; everyone loves bribes and runs after payments; the orphan they do not judge, and the quarrel of the widow does not come to them" (Is. 1:3, 23).

But the harsh rebuke of the prophet Isaiah ends with a great promise: "And I will restore your judges as at first and your counselors as in the beginning. Afterward, you shall be called City of Righteousness, Faithful City. Zion shall be redeemed through justice and her penitents through righteousness" (Is. 1:26–27).

Rebbe Levi Yitzchak of Berditchev said that on *Shabbat Ḥazon*, every Jew is given the vision to look ahead and see the Third Temple. In other words, in the midst of the days of mourning in the month of Av, this Shabbat provides encouragement with a glorious vision of the future.

Tears of hope

Netivot Shalom is the name of a wonderful series of books by Rebbe Shalom Noach Berezovsky, who passed away on the seventh of Av, 5760 (2000), two days before Tisha B'Av. Here is an excerpt highlighting his approach to proper preparation for this day:

"There are two forms of weeping: weeping that comes from despair and weeping that comes from hope. Our weeping over the destruction (of the Holy Temple) comes from hope and longing, not for what is gone but for what will be. We are not mourning what was and is no more, since the nation of Israel does not preserve memories of the past unless they are connected to the present and the future. Our mourning is a refusal to stay in the past or accept the present.

"Just as there is general redemption, there is also individual redemption. The individual is sometimes immersed in darkness, in exile, but just like general redemption, here too you must continue to believe and look forward to salvation. There are difficult and bitter states of mind in which a person feels hopeless, that he could never change. He makes peace with his reality and does not believe it can ever be improved. It is useful to heed the words of Rebbe Moshe of Karlin: 'The very worst thing is to make peace with your situation as it is.'"

TISHA B'AV
Napoleon predicts our glorious future

The mourning observed during the period "between the straits" reaches its climax on Tisha B'Av – the day the First Temple was destroyed by Nebuchadnezzar King of Babylonia, and the day the Second Temple was destroyed by Titus and the Romans. This date has become symbolic of the various catastrophes that have visited the Jewish people throughout the generations. The fast begins in the evening when we sit on the floor, read *Megillat Eikha* (Book of Lamentations) and recite elegies. We do not learn Torah on Tisha B'Av because it is considered a joyful activity that is not suited to such a sad day.

There is a famous story about Tisha B'Av involving Napoleon, who happened to be walking with his soldiers in Paris on that evening. In one of the houses he saw a crowd of people, adults and children, sitting on the floor with books in their hands, weeping bitterly. When he asked them why they were crying, they answered: "Our house burned to the ground!" Napoleon said he was surprised that such an important house could go up in flames without him hearing about it. They explained that the house had burned down two thousand years ago. Napoleon was amazed and cried out, "A nation that remembers its past so well is surely destined for a glorious future."

Who destroyed Jerusalem?

There is a poignant midrash in which Babylonia rejoices and is proud of its victory over Jerusalem. In response, Jerusalem says: "If from above, they had not made war against me, would you have been able to fight me? If from above, they had not set fire to me, would you have vanquished me?" After these questions, Jerusalem said to Babylonia: "Instead, you killed a dead lion, you ground flour that was already ground, you burned a burnt city, you destroyed a Holy Temple that was already in ruins" (Song of Songs Rabba 3:4).

This is an astonishing assertion. Babylonia simply came and plucked ripe fruit; they conquered with ease. They did not kill, burn, or destroy because everything was already destroyed, crumbled from within. The Temple was not destroyed by outside forces; any damage they did came after we ourselves had destroyed it from within. The city was not set on fire by outside forces – that happened only after we had set it on fire from within. Then and now, our enemies exploit our weaknesses. If we lack faith and motivation, if we are divided, if we forget our identity and our heritage, if we indulge the struggles of extremists and do not focus on what is essential – we are the ones who burn and destroy.

Hassan Nasrallah, leader of Hezbollah, gave a famous speech that came to be known as the "Spider Web Speech," describing Israel's disintegration from within (God forbid). Tanks and nuclear weapons are not the main threat, he said, rather it is the faith and the identity of the Israelis. Without this internal strength, they are like cobwebs. Nasrallah understood the symbolism of the ground flour and the destruction of the Temple. The question is – do we?

Understanding the magnitude of our loss

"We define the tragedy of Tisha B'Av incorrectly when we think of the Holy Temple's destruction merely as the loss of a building," writes Rabbi Yoni Lavi. "It was not just a building that was destroyed but an entirely different and unique reality. Today, we are taught to believe in something that in the past we knew and felt intrinsically. Imagine a spiritual center to which everyone's heart is connected. It is difficult to describe in words the magnitude of what we are missing when we have never experienced it. We are like poor people who do not know they are poor and do not know how rich they are supposed to be. We travel along on the ground in first gear when we are meant to be flying. We strive to experience holiness for brief moments, when Jerusalem was once a holy city for everyone, all the time.

"Today everything is upside down. Physical reality seems like absolute truth while spiritual reality is hidden. Imagine growing up in a world where marriage was nothing more than sending a weekly text message and speaking on the phone once a month. People would not know that there are other levels of connection, far deeper and more meaningful. They would not know that it is even possible to want more. Every year during the month of Av, we too need to dream, imagine, and strive for more. The month of Av is like the glass broken at our weddings that reminds us how much more we must do, that reality is not yet perfect or complete."

More than baseless hatred?

I once thought that "baseless hatred" was the only reason that the Second Temple was destroyed. This is a significant reason, but it sometimes brought me to utter empty clichés regarding unity. Indeed, sometimes we say "baseless hatred" just because it is an easy answer.

In recent years, I discovered that in the Talmud (Shabbat 119b) our Sages gave very clear reasons for the destruction of the Temple. Perhaps it is not so politically correct these days and therefore not discussed so much, but they write as follows: "Jerusalem was destroyed only because they omitted the recitation of the *Shema* in the morning and evening," "Jerusalem was destroyed only because they disparaged Torah scholars," "Jerusalem was destroyed only because schoolchildren's study of Torah was interrupted," and "Jerusalem was destroyed only because the people did not rebuke one another." Other reasons are cited that describe a society that has lost faith, respect for its identity, the ability to dialogue, and a material and spiritual concern for others.

I was a little ashamed that I did not know all the lessons our Sages learned from the destruction. Perhaps in order for the return to Zion to continue to move forward and not, heaven forbid, backward, it would be worthwhile to learn these other lessons as well.

When the Temple is destroyed

In her role as a social worker, Keren Gottlieb taught new immigrant children from Ethiopia in the Bat Hatzor caravan site near Gadera during Operation Shlomo in the 1990s. She relates the following story:

"In one of the classes, I was teaching them about the holiday of Passover and said that it is one of the three pilgrimage festivals when it was customary to go up to Jerusalem to the Holy Temple. One of the students jumped up and asked: 'Teacher, did you ever see the Holy Temple?' I smiled, thinking that he was a little confused, and explained that I was talking about something that happened a long time ago. But all the rest of the students joined him. 'Teacher, what does the Temple look like? What's it like to be there?' I tried to calm them down: 'Listen, there is no Temple. It was destroyed – burned – two thousand years ago.' The tumult in the classroom only increased. They started arguing with each other in Amharic and continued until the bell rang.

"The following morning, the guard at the school gate was shocked. He pointed to a large gathering of agitated parents. I approached the group and a man angrily asked: 'Are you the teacher? The children returned home yesterday and said you taught them that there is no Temple in Jerusalem.' I said to him: 'I just explained to them that today we do not have a Temple. What's all the fuss about?' He turned to his friends, translated the words into Amharic, and asked: 'Are you sure?' I could not hold back a smile. What a weird situation. But the man turned dramatically to his friends and resolutely translated the words. Suddenly I saw a woman fall to the ground while another began sobbing with heart-breaking tears. They began to hug one another while my students looked on with sadness and pain. I was shocked. I felt like I had delivered an unbearably tragic message to Job, as if I had told them about the death of someone they loved. I had never seen people mourn like that over the destruction of the Temple.

"Since that year, my Tisha B'Av has been completely different. I realized that this is exactly how we are supposed to mourn the Temple on Tisha B'Av. We are supposed to weep over the loss of unity and peace, to grieve the disappearance of the Divine Presence from our lives in the Land of Israel, to feel the pain of the destruction of our spiritual and cultural center around which the entire nation was united. I came to the caravans in order to teach Ethiopian immigrants but in the end, it was they who taught me a most significant lesson."

SHABBAT NAḤAMU (SABBATH OF CONSOLATION)
Seven weeks of consolation

The Shabbat after Tisha B'Av is called *Shabbat Naḥamu* after the *haftara* that begins "*Naḥamu Ami*," "Be comforted, My people" (Is. 40:1). This Shabbat is the first in a series of seven Shabbats of consolation between Tisha B'Av and Rosh HaShana, during which we read seven *haftarot* of redemption, all of them words of the prophet Isaiah.

One of the prophet's exhortations is as follows: "Rejoice with Jerusalem and be glad for her, all those who love her. Rejoice greatly with her, all who mourn over her" (Is. 66:10).

Our Sages explain: "Whoever mourns over Jerusalem will merit to see her rejoicing, and whoever does not mourn over Jerusalem will not see her rejoicing" (Taanit 30b). This is not just a prize that we will receive some day. There is a deeper lesson here: A student who did not study at all but received full marks on his exam will not feel the same triumph as the student who immersed himself in the material, studied hard, and exerted maximum effort. Someone who arrived by chance at a lavish feast and was invited to eat will not enjoy it quite as much as the one who was hungry, prepared the food, set the table, and relished the meal ahead. In order to appreciate what we have, we must feel the absence of what is missing. In order to merit authentic joy, we must participate in mourning. Whoever nurtures an emotional connection to the loss of the Holy Temple all the days of his life will know how to appreciate its rebuilding. Moreover, when we truly understand the reasons for its destruction, it becomes possible to make amends. In the Talmud, it is written that when a person ascends to the World to Come, he will be asked: "Did you actively anticipate salvation?" (Shabbat 31a). In other words, did you passively accept the situation as it was or did you strive to improve it? Did you long for redemption?

TU B'AV (FIFTEENTH OF AV)
What happened on the Fifteenth of Av?

From the saddest day of the year, Tisha B'Av, we make a sharp transition to the happiest day of the year – Tu B'Av (the Fifteenth of Av). Our Sages mention a number of uplifting events of connection and reconciliation that occurred throughout history on this day, some of them indeed correcting the distance and destruction of Tisha B'Av.

The sin of the spies took place on Tisha B'Av. They returned in despair from their excursion to the Land of Israel and persuaded the people that there was no reason to continue journeying toward it. As punishment, God decreed that that generation would die in the desert and not enter the Land of Israel. Thirty-eight years later, on the Fifteenth of Av, the dying stopped. Since then, this day has been one of joy and feasting, a date that marks the end of wandering in the desert and the beginning of preparations to enter the Land of Israel.

On the Fifteenth of Av, long after they had settled in the Land of Israel, the Sages allowed intermarriage between members of different tribes, ending the divisiveness that had resulted from not allowing such marriages. Later, on the same date, intermarriage between the tribe of Benjamin and the other tribes was also granted. It had been forbidden following the violent *pilegesh ba'giva* incident that is recorded at the end of the book of Judges (Judges 19–21).

A king of Israel by the name of Yeravam Ben Nevat split the Kingdom of Israel into Israel and Yehuda. He decreed that subjects from his kingdom (Israel) could not make pilgrimages to Jerusalem, as it was part of the Kingdom of Yehuda. This decree remained in force for generations, until it was rescinded on the Fifteenth of Av. From then on, anyone who wanted to make a pilgrimage to Jerusalem was permitted to do so. Those living in the Kingdom of Israel were now able to celebrate the three pilgrimage festivals in Jerusalem together with those from the Kingdom of Yehuda.

During the time of the Temple, felling the trees to make kindling wood for the altar was completed every year on the Fifteenth of Av, and it was considered a festive occasion. A celebration was held to honor the fulfillment and completion of the mitzva associated with supplying wood for the altar.

On Tisha B'Av, the city of Beitar was captured by the Romans. The Jews living there were massacred, but the bodies could not be brought to burial, by order of Emperor Adrianus. After years of disgraceful neglect, a new emperor arose who allowed the bodies to be brought to burial. This permission was granted on the Fifteenth of Av.

The young maidens of Jerusalem would go out to the vineyards on this day to find a match. "No days were as festive for Israel as the Fifteenth of Av and Yom Kippur" (Mishna Taanit 4:8). To this day, the Fifteenth of Av is considered the most popular date for weddings.

In kabbalistic, hasidic, and ethical works, the Fifteenth of Av is designated as the start of the process of *teshuva*, coming half a month before the beginning of Elul. Some have the custom to begin soul-searching on this day since the nights are lengthening and nighttime Torah study increases. Some also have the custom of beginning to wish others the traditional blessing before Yom Kippur: "May you be inscribed and sealed (in the Book of Life)."

All these events comprise an abbreviated history of mourning and rejoicing that is woven together in our history, and the Fifteenth of Av highlights our moments of consolation.

The secret to sixty years of happy marriage

Rabbi Professor Benjamin Bloch from New York celebrated sixty years of marriage to his wife Elaine, and shared some words of advice for the secret to a good marriage:

"Many people have asked me recently to reveal our secret, and I told them that actually, the secret is one I learned the first time I studied Talmud as a child. The most famous case that children learn first is called *shenayim oḥazin*, 'two people are clutching,' in which two people are clutching a tallit. 'One says, "It's mine," and the other says, "It's mine."' The court's ruling is finally given: They must divide it between themselves. No one gets all he wants; they must learn to share. It is interesting that this particular discussion is the introduction to talmudic discourse for young children. It leaves a lasting impression on the young mind of the Jewish child: not everything is yours, you are not the center of the universe, you must learn to compromise, and you must be sensitive toward the needs and wants of others.

"In a world of maximum self-gratification, of selfies, of 'I deserve it,' it seems that the key words that motivate people today are 'everything is mine.' No one wants to be considered a loser, not even a little, not even for a moment. After sixty years of a happy marriage, my recommendation is not to say, 'This is mine' but rather, 'This is ours.' Ultimately, this will not result in you losing half. Almost miraculously, both partners will instead gain so much more. I am happy to share with you this insight that is easy to learn in the Talmud but more complicated to apply in life."

"... According to the law of Moses and Israel"

During *Sheva Berakhot* in honor of the marriage of Oshri Yosipov and Nir Levi, the groom, Nir, shared some reflections with those gathered on Shabbat morning:

"Under the ḥuppa, before placing the ring on Oshri's finger, I said the words, 'Behold, you are consecrated to me with this ring, according to the law of Moses and Israel.' Why this choice of words? It is clear that we, like every couple, wanted to get married according to the law of Moses and Israel, just like our ancestors did before us. But what is the meaning of the words 'according to the law of Moses and Israel,' aside from being another link in the chain of continuity from one generation to the next?

"One of the beautiful answers that Oshri and I found is that the nation of Israel and Moses walked together in the desert for forty years. There were ups and downs, successes and failures, but they did not separate. They continued together because they shared the same path and had a common purpose. The same is true of marriage. Not every moment is like the moments under the *ḥuppa*. There are many challenges. But as we establish our home, we announce that our lives will be conducted 'according to the law of Moses and Israel.' We want our relationship to be like that of Moses and the people of Israel, with an enormous love that overcame all difficulties between them. We hope that our common goal will give us strength, and that like Moses and Israel, we will not stop praying, hoping, and improving throughout the years."

Making room for God

It is not certain that "the Jewish Valentine's Day" or "Holiday of Love" is the appropriate name for the Fifteenth of Av. Perhaps "Festival of Marriage" or "Celebration of Worthy Investment" would be more appropriate. Rabbi Netanel Elyashiv gave the following message to a young couple under the *ḥuppa*:

"Love is great, but it is not everything. Of course the partner you choose is important, but no less important is the meaning of marriage. When a couple understands that their connection is more than the sum of their own individual needs but centers around a common purpose, it gives their relationship and everything they do together the right perspective.

"Let's use an example from the army: Within any group of soldiers, there are different types of people, but it is rare that there is ongoing discord among them. Were you to put the same people in a civilian setting, things could be very different, and they could even have an explosive falling out. Why does the situation affect their relationship? Because in the army they have a common purpose, and this minimizes the potential for destructive behavior from the very beginning. When everything is built solely on love and feelings, the relationship rests on a shaky foundation, since feelings are fickle and unreliable. In addition to feelings and emotions, which are of course essential, being enveloped in spirituality and longing for closeness to God brings meaning to raising children and all other aspects of married life. With this as your foundation, as a married couple you will think twice before speaking hurtful words, and you will also quickly make amends. There is no alternative, since your lives will be spent working together toward the same purpose. Therefore, when we make room in our home for the Holy One, blessed be He, there is actually more room – and peace – for everyone."

Ten Commandments of dating

The following are ten insights on dating, taken from the writings of the Lubavitcher Rebbe, collected by Maayanotekha, a publisher of hasidic works:

- **Seek and you shall find.** Even though there is much room for faith, patience, and prayers, there is no substitute for the search itself, for going on dates again and again without losing hope. As the Rebbe wrote in a letter to a young woman who despaired from the wearisome process of dating: "You must keep trying again and again. In the end, it is certain that you will find a proper partner, but there is no doubt that the process demands effort and hard work."

- **Stop living in fantasy land.** Many young people imagine marriage as something that does not necessarily exist. Love and devotion will grow, but first you must find a life partner. The following words were written by the Lubavitcher Rebbe to a young woman who wrote that she had gone out with many young men but was not attracted to any of them: "You have been overly influenced by romance novels. In reality, even when someone meets a fitting partner, there is not always a flash of lightning or butterflies in your stomach. That happens in a fantasy and comes from an imaginary world with imaginary feelings. When two people meet, a thin bond may form between them, like a small flame. The flame is a feeling that grows and strengthens over the years until it becomes a raging fire, whose fuel is cooperation, caring, mutual respect, shared challenges, overcoming obstacles, and creating a warm family unit in the home. Ultimately, a point is reached where two people who started out almost as strangers cannot imagine living without each other."

- **Focus on what matters.** When there is hesitation, we need to shine a light on what matters and not become small-minded. "It is impossible to find someone perfect in all respects, and it is impossible to take account of everything. If the things that matter are there, it is appropriate to ignore minor matters that appear unsuitable since they may anyway be imagined."

- **Don't get stuck in the past.** The Lubavitcher Rebbe often said that a long delay in finding a marriage partner may be associated with a prior relationship that ended badly. The Rebbe insisted that every relationship end pleasantly and honorably, without anger or resentment toward the other person.

- **Listen to your parents, too.** Despite the individualism that rules in this generation, it is worth considering the valuable advice and judgment of parents who raised their children into adulthood. "Your father and mother most definitely want what is best for you and to be of assistance in any way they can. And since it is sometimes difficult to make a life-changing decision, it would be worthwhile to consult with the people who know you best."

- **Don't marry someone you think you can change.** Despite the sincere desire to "help" someone move forward in life, the Lubavitcher Rebbe was opposed to a marriage based on the latent "potential" of a chosen partner. We must look at someone as he or she is right now and consider whether that person is good for us with all their pros and cons. In the Rebbe's words: "It is understood, of course, that a *shid-dukh* (match) is not about educating or changing another person, but rather about building a home in Israel on the foundations of Jewish tradition with someone whose outlook on life is similar to yours."

- **Don't date anyone for too long.** It is not good to be in a relationship for a long time without a commitment. Both partners need to consider whether they are ready to establish a home.

- **A time-out can be beneficial.** How do you know if your attraction to someone is genuine, that there is love, that this person is meant to be your partner for life? The Lubavitcher Rebbe gave a simple suggestion on several occasions when this question arose: Separate and cut off contact for a certain period of time. If each heart longs for the other, it's the real thing. "It is advisable not to meet for a while. This lack of contact will accentuate your feelings, whether positive or negative."

- **Use both the head and the heart.** The decision is made neither by the heart alone, nor by the mind alone. "The decision needs to come from both the head and the heart, but sometimes what appears to be a rational thought is actually an emotion...and so the matter must be carefully considered."

- **Think of your friends.** "Start by prioritizing finding matches for your friends, and in doing so, you will find your own."

On humor and a common purpose

If we take a moment to look beyond the fanfare and commercialism that sometimes characterizes Tu B'Av, we find one of the most exciting, difficult, yet rewarding challenges that we as humans can experience – that of building a relationship, a home, a family.

Here are two pieces of advice from different worlds for anyone facing this challenge, one from a rabbi and one taken from a well-known author:

Rabbi Shlomo Wolbe once received a letter from a worried woman, a mother and wife, who laid out her troubles before him. The solution to her problems could be summed up in one word: humor. He advised her to become "skilled in humor." We tend to lose control, he explained. We get into arguments, magnify little things regarding our spouse and children, and don't relate to them appropriately. A smile, a good word, a light touch, the ability to look at what's happening at home with amusement – this is the best medicine for what ails you, he told her, instead of exaggerating and taking every little thing so seriously. He concluded that it is specifically those who are connected to eternal values who are best able to make use of humor.

Antoine de Saint-Exupéry, author of *The Little Prince*, was once asked what love is. He answered: "Love is not two people gazing lovingly into each other's eyes. Love is two people looking forward together toward a common goal." In other words, love is not only about satisfying our romantic needs but also about having a common vision, purpose, and direction in life.

Humor and purpose – both are necessary for a successful relationship. Have a happy Tu B'Av!

Days of Corona

PANDEMIC

In December 2019 (5780), the initial outbreak of COVID-19 occurred in Wuhan, China. Within a few months, it began to spread rapidly throughout the world, changing the face of humanity. Millions died, more than 100 million were infected, and a severe financial crisis ensued. The daily routine of the entire world was interrupted when educational, religious, and cultural institutions were shuttered, businesses folded, airports closed, and nearly all social events and gatherings were canceled. "Mask," "social distancing," "lockdown," "curfew," "isolation," "morbidity rate," and "Zoom" were features of a new language that suddenly became part of our daily vocabulary.

In February 2021 (5781), a new series of more infectious mutations of the virus began to develop, even while a massive worldwide vaccination campaign began, in which Israel prominently led the way.

This chapter is a collection of articles that were published during the first year of the COVID-19 pandemic. It appears here in the hope that we will soon be reading it as history, and no longer part of our daily lives.

Every contact has an effect

The panic surrounding the outbreak of COVID-19 brought Chani Lifshitz, Chabad emissary in Katmandu, Nepal, to write the following:

"Suddenly we need to think very carefully: Which route did we take? Which people were in our area? How long were we in the presence of those people? Do we recall other people who passed by, and their exact proximity? Did we shake their hands, embrace one another?

"Honestly, how many of us have ever stopped to think about such things when it is not about COVID-19? One day quickly follows another, but suddenly we are asked to stop, to understand how critical it is to remember every detail about people we happened to meet along the way. This short encounter could have a major impact on our lives. Suddenly it becomes clear how great the long-term effect of any encounter with another person can be, however brief and unimportant it may seem. We should never think for a moment that any contact we make with another is arbitrary. Indeed, we have seen now that it can stay within our body and soul for many days, changing our lives from one extreme to the other, for better or for worse. One can infect another who infects another, and on and on it continues. So it is in this world; we are all dependent upon each other. The effect of every action can be felt from one end of the earth to the other. Then there are those who need to quarantine. Physically isolated as they are from other people, they have the opportunity for some reflection and introspection. I am sure that when they are released from quarantine, they will have a new appreciation for the energy created when two people meet."

Embracing uncertainty

"We learned many lessons this past year while our daughter battled leukemia," Rabbi Zalman Vishetzky writes from Basel, Switzerland.

"There were painful crash courses in topics such as 'How to be happy even in an oncology department,' 'How to preserve your marriage when your child has a life-threatening illness,' and 'How to relate to your other children when one of them is desperately ill.' But the most meaningful course was 'How to live with uncertainty.' It was impossible to plan anything. For example, in the morning our daughter would feel well, and two hours later she would feel sick. In the afternoon she was at home and in the evening she was in the hospital. For how long? No one knew. We were used to planning everything, and then suddenly everything was up in the air.

"It takes a little while until you realize that this is precisely the lesson to be learned: to accept uncertainty with a calm smile. After fearing the unexpected, you learn to embrace it. You learn to let go, to be thankful for what you have, and to wholeheartedly put your time, your money, and your destiny in the hands of Hashem."

Rabbi Vishetzky's daughter recovered, thank God, and this week he wanted to send a message to all of us: "Amidst the enormous chaos of COVID-19, there is one thing that is very clear: Everything is uncertain. Many people have lost their jobs. Those who made reservations to spend the Passover holiday in hotels in Italy are beginning to clean their houses. Those who are about to get married don't know who will make it to the wedding hall. That is all to say nothing of the fear of being infected. All of us are now learning the lesson of 'How to live with uncertainty.' From my experience, to succeed in this course you need to open your heart and embrace the unexpected. Turn the uncertainty you are feeling now into the certainty that comes from allowing yourself to rely on Hashem no matter what."

A guide for the isolated

"Excuse me sir, why are you not leaving your home?" Rabbi Shmuel Volk asked his readers in the weekly newsletter *Az Nidbaru*. "Why are you sequestered in your room? The real reason, I think, is like this: There is a very tiny chance that your young child is infected with the virus, and then maybe-maybe you are infected, and then maybe-maybe-maybe you will infect others, and then maybe-maybe-maybe-maybe they will get sick – and therefore, because of this miniscule possibility, you stay at home.

"In other words, you are now missing daily prayers in synagogue and forgoing many other things solely to protect your neighbor's health. You may not even be particularly fond of this neighbor normally, yet in the moment of truth you realize that his life is more important than all your prayers and comforts. Have you ever thought of it this way?

"So during the difficult hours of isolation, I suggest we declare with all our hearts: 'Master of the universe, what am I not willing to do in order to protect Your people? I am stuck here in isolation solely to prevent me from possibly transmitting the virus, even though that possibility may be tiny. If I sinned against You with baseless hatred of others, if I once mistakenly said something negative about one of Your people, all of whom are dear to You, let this isolation be a sign of sincere contrition and regret for what I did.'"

A sense of proportion

"Hi Sivan, my name is Leah. Yesterday I saw some hysterical women next to the empty shelves in the supermarket, behaving in a way that frightened their children. Like everyone, I am inundated with 'fake news' day and night on WhatsApp, complete with lots of exclamation marks. COVID-19 is infectious, but so is the panic surrounding it, and it is equally dangerous.

"I am considered one of the elderly. Everyone is in lockdown because of us, in order to protect us from getting sick, so thank you all. However, it seems to me that we can help you with something too, and that is keeping a sense of proportion. If there is one thing that our society needs right now it is mature, stable people with inner strength and resilience. Children need to see functioning, authoritative parents who convey confidence even in these new and uncertain circumstances.

"I came to Israel from Europe after the Holocaust. I was here [during the wars] in '48, '67, and '73. We experienced days of hunger and austerity, shortages, and panic. Believe me, the way that we react is important. If we make an effort, we may even be able to get through this current crisis with a smile. There are graphs that show the number of those infected, but there is no graph showing faith and confidence. There is a wonderful verse in the book of Psalms: 'Let go and know that I am God' (Ps. 46:11). It would be worthwhile repeating these words every now and then."

What is normal?

At the beginning of the first lockdown, Rabbi Yoni Lavi published the following thought-provoking article:

"This is not normal," my wife said. "Everything is shut down, it's impossible to meet anyone, and the kids are stuck inside all day. This situation with corona just isn't normal."

"You are a hundred percent right," I agreed with her. "What's going on here is completely abnormal. But on the other hand, constantly running around and living with permanent stress – is that normal?

"Going through twenty-four hours when you hardly remember where you were, whom you met, and whose hand you shook – is that normal?

"Only letting other people clean your house and teach your kids – is that normal?

"Flying abroad frequently, signing up for attractive deals to spend Passover Seder in Egypt or Hanukka in Greece – is that normal?

"Going out every other day to eat when the food they serve you is processed, full of fat, cholesterol, and sugar – is that normal?

"Throwing huge sums of money to host an 'amaaaazing' wedding or bar/bat mitzva for hundreds of guests, complete with all the trimmings – is that normal?

"Running around at huge public events among countless strangers, with little time left over for the love of your life and your sweet children – is that normal?

"I hope that perhaps when the pandemic is over, we will learn to live a more balanced life."

The moment of truth

"These are days of fear and mysticism," writes Rabbi Chagai Londin from the Hesder Yeshiva (where Torah learning is combined with IDF service) in Sderot. "Every few years, the general public and each of us individually face some sort of danger: a natural disaster, economic collapse, war, or a troubling disease or medical condition. The way we cope with fear is directly determined by our spiritual outlook. Controlling our imagination is an essential component of our spiritual development. There is no point in getting carried away with mystical calculations where the *Gematria* (numerical value of Hebrew letters) of 'corona' is the same as 'Gog and Magog at the end of days,' or exaggerating and saying that the world is about to end.

"We need to heed the directives of the Ministry of Health with the utmost diligence. Beyond this, most of us can do nothing, and therefore the best thing to do is to continue to engage in what is beneficial to our lives and not waste time on baseless rumors that only deepen our anxiety. More important than everything else is prayer because the foundation of a positive attitude is faith in God. A clear mind vanquishes all dark imaginings and apprehensions.

"The end of the world is not coming now, and indeed will never come, because faith teaches us that this world is good. Moreover, God provides human beings with intelligence, with the ability and the courage to meet every challenge. Keeping calm and demonstrating optimism, discretion, common sense, courage, stability, and faith – these are the values with which to nurture our souls in the 21st century.

"The day will come, and it's not far off, when the COVID-19 crisis will be behind us. And then the moment will arrive in which we will face our children, our friends, ourselves, and especially our Father in heaven, and answer the question of how we functioned in this time of crisis. Did we lose our cool, were we filled with despair, did we radiate pessimism and belittle the restrictions, incite grumbling, show frustration, and sow panic, or did we do what was expected of us, strictly abiding by the guidelines, showing concern for others, and demonstrating faith, confidence, and a sense of proportion?

"People of both types have existed throughout history: in ancient times, in the Middle Ages, during both World Wars, during the Yom Kippur War, in the time of financial crises, and when those precious to us were stricken with a devastating disease. I wish we could all answer that we were of the second, optimistic type. The word "*Yehudi*" (Jew) is derived from "*hodaa*" (gratitude). Our Sages teach: 'A person is obligated to bless the bad just as he blesses the good' (Mishna Berakhot 9:5). God is always here, even when times are hard – especially when times are hard.

"Now is the moment of truth. Let us stand up to the challenge."

Apathy adds to our suffering

During the pandemic, we have prayed time and again to return to the life that we enjoyed previously. However, Maimonides writes that when faced with such a severe decree, a decree that threatens the entire world, we should not desire to simply go back to the way things were before as if nothing had changed. We need to see the suffering and distress as an incentive for improvement, and to understand the lesson that is hidden in such a difficult time.

"It is a positive commandment from the Torah to cry out and to sound trumpets for all troubles that come upon the community," Maimonides writes. "That is to say, with every matter that troubles you, such as famine, plague, locusts, and similar ills, cry out about them and sound the trumpets. This is one of the paths to repentance."

What is the alternative, if we ignore and remain indifferent to what is happening, if we do not improve ourselves and society? Maimonides continues: "But if they do not cry out and sound [trumpets], but rather say, 'This is the way of the world, and this trouble is merely happenstance,' it is surely a destructive way of thinking, causing them to stick to their corrupt ways, and then more troubles will befall them." (*Mishneh Torah, Hilkhot Taaniyot* [Fasts] 1:1–3).

According to Maimonides, we are not supposed to just keep our heads down and wait for the pandemic to pass, but rather we must raise our heads to look for the lessons we can learn from it and change our behavior accordingly.

A "Corona Shabbat"

I heard someone say: "We are in lockdown – all week we sat at home and did nothing, so what's the big deal about Shabbat now? The whole week was one long Shabbat."

If Shabbat is only about sitting around and doing nothing – she's right. But in my opinion she is mistaken. All week long, the word "no" seemed to appear in the news more and more – no buses, no flights, no schools, no coffee shops. You can't do this and you can't do that. There is no doubt that COVID-19 struck us hard during the week. But this evening we have Shabbat. Now we have the opportunity to say "yes." Yes to Shabbat candles, yes to Kiddush, yes to a special dinner, yes to family togetherness.

Not another twenty-four hours spent scrolling through endless, frightening news briefs, but a completely different twenty-four hours where we disconnect in order to connect. We are compelled to stay at home, but Shabbat does not need to be the same as the rest of the week.

I do not know if there have ever been so many closed synagogues in the history of the Jewish people, so many people not able to say *Kaddish* or read from a Torah scroll. These challenging health measures must be followed with utmost care, but perhaps our mission this Shabbat is to bring the holiness of the synagogue into our living room and kitchen.

Shabbat shalom.

Between distance and unity

Amidst the initial outbreak of the COVID-19 pandemic and just a few months before he passed away, Rabbi Lord Jonathan Sacks was invited to the BBC studios in London to address the British nation. Below are some of the points he made. I pray that his optimistic predictions will ultimately come true:

"Bad events like the coronavirus – the worst certainly in my lifetime – do sometimes bring out the worst in us, but they also bring out the best. Right now...there are groups of people circulating among the elderly and vulnerable, saying: 'Can I help?' ...As time passes, we will see more and more of this. Supermarkets are gearing up to provide basic supplies. Young people are preparing to deliver medicines to people in need.... We are going to see a renewal of the 'we'....

"We have talked far too much about rights, and far too little about responsibilities. And what we are seeing is people being willing to handle their responsibilities. And I don't know why we let it slip out of the discourse because it's an essential part. Without responsibilities, in the end, you'll find you have no rights....

"At present, we are distant physically, but in a certain sense we are very united. I think that our scattered focus, where each person is looking at something different, is about to change. At the moment, all of us are looking at the same news, more or less, and are reacting in pretty much the same way. Although physically we cannot be together, mentally and emotionally, I think we will be....

"I don't know when we've been more embraced, every one of us in a vital and personal way with this huge circle of humanity. I don't know when all the countries of the world have simultaneously faced the same danger. Just a few weeks ago we could say this is happening to someone else, somewhere else, a half a world away. All of a sudden, it's now affecting every one of us....

"We will never forget this period, the way people never forgot the Second World War. I didn't know how my parents kept remembering that war as if that was such a vivid moment in their lives, but they did because when you face a danger, and you face it together with lots of other people, it becomes incredibly vivid and personality-shaping in terms of your memory. So I think this is going to change every one of us.... For many decades we lived with unprecedented affluence, freedom, and optimism, but now we are suddenly reminded of the fragility of the human situation.

"What we are now experiencing is the closest thing we have to divine revelation, a revelation of the inescapable link of humanity. I think this is going to change every one of us. I think we will emerge from this as better people, with a stronger sense of identification with others and our responsibility toward them."

Miriam Peretz: Shabbat alone

Miriam Peretz posted a photo of her Shabbat table: One plate, grape juice, challah, and a Kiddush cup. That was it. She complied with the safety measures in this way. After Shabbat, she was interviewed and said:

"I had a wonderful Shabbat. I never cook for myself – I always think about what the grandchildren like to eat – so this time I prepared kasha for myself. That is something my grandchildren don't eat. We are a Moroccan family and they would ask, 'What is this?' So I made kasha for myself, just for fun.

"Moments of crisis are not meant to break us. It's not just an expression that a woman giving birth 'dwells in crisis.' She feels pain, but from within the pain a child is born. Moments of crisis are moments you can take for some introspection, and to ask questions that there is no time to ask during the craziness of daily life. Last Shabbat, when I read the words alone from the psalm that we say before Kiddush, I was suddenly enlightened by the phrase: 'Although I walk through the valley of the shadow of death, I will fear no evil since You are with me' (Ps. 23:4). 'I will fear no evil,' I said to myself, and I was strengthened. Life throws us into all kinds of situations, but we choose how to interpret them. You can translate the current situation into the thought that you are alone and isolated, or you can say, 'I am giving this moment to myself as a gift.'

"And in any case, what would a person not do to stay alive? If they tell us to take a certain medicine in order to live, we take it. But now all they are saying is: 'Sit at home and you will live.' So this will last for a while – the main thing is to look ahead and ask, 'Why am I alone?' And the answer is: so that I will once again be able to open my Shabbat table to thirty people, as always, and once again hear Kiddush with all my children and grandchildren."

A private synagogue under my kitchen window

"Shalom, my name is Dalit, and I live in central Israel. The last time I set foot in a synagogue was for my brother's bar mitzva years ago, but now everything has changed. We have heard for weeks about people whose synagogues were closed, but not about the prayer services that have sprung up in the streets, under kitchen windows of people like me. At first, I was angry at the people who had started praying below. I was even planning to complain about them. But over time, their praying became part of my daily rhythm and

I have even begun to like it. I do not pray with them, but I notice that the sun comes up with their morning prayers and I know that tomorrow will start the same way, both for them and for me. And I see how the sun goes down during their afternoon prayers and how the stars come out with their evening prayers. Sometimes I even answer 'Amen' when they say *Kaddish*.

"The highlight, of course, is Shabbat. Their prayer is slower and full of songs. I did not know most of the tunes at first, but now I know them well and even find myself humming them during the week: '*Lecha dodi likrat kallah* ....'

"There is no kitschy ending to this story. I don't think I will start going to synagogue when the pandemic is over, and I did not even go down to say 'thank you' to those whose prayers I enjoyed listening to. They don't know that I was with them when they prayed. But now that everyone is talking about easing restrictions and returning to normal life, I am happy of course, but also a little sad that the private synagogue under my kitchen window will soon be closed."

A baby naming at the end of the world

"Hi Sivan. I believe this story is worth publicizing. My name is Dror Proctor, and I am an emissary of Torah MiTzion in Perth, Australia. The COVID-19 situation here is very good, thank God, and we are able to pray in a regular *minyan* at the Carmel Jewish school. Several days ago, a little girl was born in Baltimore, Maryland to a family we did not know. The parents, Ari and Sara Stern, were not able to give her a name in their synagogue because they are still in lockdown. They searched for a place somewhere in the world that still has a regular *minyan*, and they reached us. It was an amazing day! The parents were with us in a video call throughout the prayer service, with forty students in a school at one end of the world rejoicing and praying for a baby girl born on the other side of the world. These students were the first to hear the baby's name, joyfully dancing and singing '*Siman tov umazal tov*' when it was announced, 'And her name in Israel shall be: Liba.'

"This was a moment we shall never forget. We speak a lot about solidarity and how we are all part of the same human tapestry. We speak about the deep connection we have with every Jew. But it takes an event like this to evoke that special feeling no words can describe."

How do we return to the synagogue?

Between one lockdown and the next, the opening of synagogues was permitted, albeit with restrictions. Rabbi Avinadav Abukarat wrote the following to his congregation at the Avnei HaHoshen Synagogue in Givat Shmuel:

"It is difficult to describe how good it is to come out of the destruction that we have experienced during the past months. I do not hesitate to use the word 'destruction,' with the loss of livelihood for many of us, the sickness and pain among weak and vulnerable populations, and the undermining of family and community life. But after all the destructions in the history of our people, buildings were rebuilt. Every time our world was shattered, people resettled and started over again. At this time, I would like to suggest one way of building anew, by strengthening synagogue prayer:

"First, our prayer needs to be more uplifting and more precise. They say that Rabbi Yinon Hori, after a prolonged sickness, would go from one *minyan* to the next at the Itzkovitch synagogue (*minyanim* are held there around the clock) in Bnei Brak to seek out opportunities to repeat Kaddish and amen, making up for the ones he missed during his illness. Not everyone is able to say the additional Kaddish or amen, but all of us can try harder to increase our concentration when praying and to take greater care in preserving the holiness of the synagogue.

"We must not allow ourselves to come back to the synagogue as if we had only left it yesterday. We have longed to return not only to the synagogue but to Torah classes, to community prayer, and to reading from a Torah scroll, and so we must not let this longing go to waste. We must return to synagogue prayer with deep appreciation for the reminder we were given of the community's importance. Let's take advantage of this opportunity for return and renewal in order to draw closer to Hashem and to the members of our community. Let's not return to the synagogue with hesitation or confusion, with apathy or out of habit. Let's return with a feeling of elevation, raising our voices with indomitable strength."

When Aviv Geffen cried

Singer Aviv Geffen came for a television interview about the protest of performing artists against the COVID-19 ban on their appearances. Instead of discussing that issue, Aviv suddenly made headlines when he tearfully recounted a recent event. This moment became one of the most talked-about and emotional events in the first wave of COVID-19 in Israel.

He explained that in the early days of the pandemic, he performed alone in a live broadcast without an audience at the amphitheater in Binyamina, and dedicated a heartfelt song to the residents of Bnei Brak who were suffering huge losses from the virus while at the same time being subjected to ugly attacks (in response to some of the city's residents violating lockdown measures).

"I leave the stage," Aviv said, "and I see on my telephone, without exaggeration, 420 messages. I start opening them, scrolling, and learn that someone had given my number to all of Bnei Brak. And I cried. I could not leave the empty amphitheater. The love, the division in the nation – suddenly everything came together. The love I received came from people I had denigrated since I was nineteen years old and who were now responding with love and tears. 'Thank you so much Aviv for thinking of us,' I read. I was just sitting on the stairs, the place was empty, and I was reading the messages and crying. At four in the morning, the theater staff got me up and told me, 'Go home.'"

The interviewer, Dana Weiss, wondered why Aviv cried then and why he was crying now. This is what he answered: "For years we learned how to hate the other. *He's religious. He's secular.* I too was a soldier in this game. Suddenly I saw the other. You ask: So how did COVID-19 change me? Just like this: I learned to respect. A flame of love, simply amazing, was lit. I cannot even describe it in words, only in tears."

Learning to be patient

It is easier to live with either total lockdown or total freedom. The hardest part is striking a balance, and that is what is required of us now – to adhere to the daily guidelines of the Health Ministry. Julius Caesar is famous for his arrogant declaration, "I came, I saw, I conquered." From then until now, we seek to win with a single knock-out blow. Rabbi Itamar Haikin, an educator at the Ruah HaSadeh pre-military academy, wrote the following regarding such impatience.

"We have difficulty coping with a lengthy process that demands restraint and patience. We once had a war that was over in six days, and since then it seems to us that this is the nature of all wars. We prefer a quick start-up over building a large company in the long term. It seems everything should happen in one fell swoop. We move speedily between emotional extremes, which is why it is so difficult for us to cope with the COVID-19 pandemic which requires forbearance. It appears that it will be here with us for a long time, yet we are already fed up. In the real world we win with small points and small victories, accompanied by small setbacks. The world advances little by little and we need to be prepared for hard work and perseverance. We are not running a sprint, but a marathon. It would seem that we in Israeli society must undergo a deep spiritual change. It was stated long ago by our Sages: 'Such is the redemption of Israel – little by little' (Y. Berakhot 1:1). Our redemption depends on overcoming our characteristic impatience, on learning the secret of deep, long breaths, on understanding that progress is made little by little, drop by drop."

Zoom with Jerusalem

Rabbi Avi Berman, executive director of the OU (Orthodox Union) organization in Israel, asked every Israeli to seek out one Jew he knows in the Diaspora and give him a call. He said that if we just "pick up the telephone" (or send a message on What-sApp!) we can do wonders. Try this: "How are you? I heard the news about what is happening in Italy/Britain/Spain/America and I am thinking of you here in Israel." You will not believe the emotional emojis such a simple message will produce.

I understood the power of the connection between us and the intensity of the longing for Israel during a Zoom discussion I had with the Kemp Mill Synagogue community in Maryland (in the United States). I had prepared a full lecture and at the end asked if there were any questions. Devorah, one of the participants, raised her hand and spoke with deep emotion: "I want to tell you the truth. I did not listen to a single word of your lecture. I couldn't concentrate. I was not in Israel for Passover, although I wanted to be there. Afterward we thought we would come for Yom HaAtzma'ut or Shavuot. When that didn't happen, we were sure we would be there in July or August, but now it turns out we won't even make it for the High Holy Days. We miss it so much. So when I heard a little while ago that there was a Zoom meeting with an Israeli, I immediately joined, if only to be connected for one hour with the Land of Israel through you. I don't have any questions. I only wanted to say that Israel is the home of every Jew in the world, and I haven't been home for far too long."

A sanctuary in every situation

Since the beginning of the corona crisis, my family has lived in four different homes on two continents. We returned from our mission to the United States, lived out of suitcases, rented apartments, and eventually, thank God, found our place. Perhaps for this reason, I immediately connected with what educator Aviah Sadeh wrote to me about her tenth grade students at a girls' boarding school in Even Shmuel.

"Every day there are new directives. Not all the girls can stay every night in the dormitory; they have to attend school on different days and keep changing their dorm rooms and classrooms. Every week we try to predict which students will arrive and which ones will be learning on Zoom, but for all of us it is difficult to plan ahead. Girls who ask for their exact schedule hear the following Torah verse which has now become our standard refrain: 'At the bidding of the Lord they traveled, and at the bidding of the Lord, they encamped' (Num. 9:18).

"These words are a wonderful description of the children of Israel wandering in the desert, and they give the girls and myself strength during these days that seem like a long journey. Sometimes the children of Israel set up camp for a short period of time, and other times they stayed much longer. Sometimes it was comfortable to stay in the same place and other times there was a desire to move on, but they were forced to remain where they were. But wherever they stopped, they immediately set up the Mishkan (portable Sanctuary), the heart of the camp – even if the very next day they would be forced to take it down, pack it up, and move on. Even after they had passed through many encampments and were weary, they never forgot the purpose of the journey. Wherever or whenever they stopped, they always focused on the main thing, the work of erecting the Mishkan, no matter what the surrounding circumstances might be. Just like they did then, so we do now, exercising our flexibility muscle on our journey, trying to bring out the best in each other at every stop along the way."

Celebrating a bar/bat mitzva during a pandemic

What do you say to bat mitzva girls who have waited twelve years for a celebration, only for it to be canceled and transformed into a family meal? What do you say to bar mitzva boys who are accepting upon themselves the yoke of Torah and mitzvot with so little fanfare? I have heard several wise thoughts on this subject from teachers and parents:

- **"First of all, make room for the pain."** A child psychologist explained to me that it is easier to ignore the disappointment and say, "The main thing is that we are all healthy," or "We will make you a beautiful birthday next year." It is easier to send a message that this is not a big deal, that it's just one less party. But the children have dreamed and planned, their imaginations have taken flight, and often a hall has already been reserved and guests invited. Instead of pushing the canceled event aside and ploughing forward, it is worth allowing a place for frustration and sadness, even tears.

- **"We saved thousands of shekels on a bat mitzva bash."** It may not be pleasant to admit, but many parents breathed a sigh of relief that the overly expensive, glitzy party was avoided. They had a small celebration with family and close friends and felt that the experience was far more meaningful than it would have been otherwise. No amount of money could have bought the fulfillment they experienced from their low-key event. This is an opportunity to open a discussion on the character of Bar and bat mitzva events in general, not just during the pandemic. Where did we get the ideas of riding in a limousine, hiring expensive pop singers, or a bar mitzva boy jumping out of a cake? It is not only a matter of the money that is spent, but the message that is conveyed. As with weddings, here too the pandemic has compelled all of us to transition to a mindset of "walking humbly" (Mic. 6:8) and we may all be happy to continue in this manner.

- **"When all else is canceled, the mitzva still remains."** When all the "extras" are canceled, when there are fewer guests and presents and less of a performance, it is possible to focus on what is most important. It is not by chance that a girl is called a bat (literally, daughter) mitzva and a boy a bar (literally, son) mitzva. All other relationships can be severed. An employee can resign, a soldier can finish his army service, and unfortunately, even a marriage can end. But the relationship between parents and children cannot be severed, no matter what. We hope our children will feel the same way regarding the relationship with their identity and their tradition – that they will always feel close, like a son or a daughter, in a strong and eternal bond that cannot be severed.

- **"This is a first lesson in becoming an adult."** This is the essence of life as an adult: knowing how to cope with disappointments, not breaking down but learning from them. A vast number of children have now encountered a difficult challenge for the first time in their lives, precisely at the moment they celebrate becoming adults. And this is perhaps the greatest gift they can receive: accepting mitzvot into their lives at the time of a pandemic, learning about commitment despite adversity and growing stronger in the process.

Creative kindness

This is one of the most moving stories I heard during the pandemic:

An elderly widow in Brooklyn realized that she would have to hold her Passover Seder alone. One of her neighbors offered to place his Seder table next to the entrance to his apartment and keep the door open so that she could hear the entire Seder from her apartment. And so it was. She opened her door and heard every word coming from her neighbor's Seder table.

The following night, her son called and asked how her Seder had been. "Wonderful," his mother said. "I felt completely at home. It was interesting how my neighbor conducted his Seder exactly as your father, of blessed memory, conducted it. The same style, the same melodies, the same customs. The melodies brought back wonderful memories."

"Mother," her son said. "Now I understand what your neighbor was up to. He called me a week ago and asked me to record for him all of our family's Seder melodies and provide details of all our customs."

This is far more than normal kindness. It is creative kindness, on a higher, deeper level. In the lead-up to Passover, during those hectic days when COVID-19 was running rampant and wreaking havoc, this is what concerned the neighbor of an elderly lady. Not only to take her into consideration and kindly open his door to her, but to have her feel as uplifted as possible during her Seder.

Much more than choosing napkins

What do we say to all the couples getting married during the pandemic in a manner that is so different from the wedding of their dreams?

We can say, first of all, that the pandemic is temporary but the marriage bond is eternal. The devastation of the pandemic will pass, while the positive influence of building a Jewish home will last forever. Perhaps the exhausting masterclass of "How to make a wedding in the middle of a pandemic" is the best training for married life. After this crazy beginning, all the "usual" trials of life that come later may be easy in comparison. Before the wedding, often some of the biggest issues couples have to contend with are choosing napkin colors and flower arrangements, but now many couples have navigated upheavals and challenges before their wedding that even long-married couples have not experienced. There are couples who, just days before their wedding, still don't know where the wedding will be held and how many guests they can invite. There are couples who have had to postpone their wedding date, change their banquet hall, and cancel hundreds of wedding invitations. Wedding invitations are printed now with only the couple's names and the date of the wedding, no other details, because they only know one, essential component – they have chosen to build a home together.

It is said that at the first wedding in history, the wedding of Adam and Eve, there weren't any guests. So God Himself arrived in all His glory to gladden the hearts of the couple. The feeling now, during our corona weddings, is somewhat the same: the number of guests may be few, but there is a special sanctity in the air.

It is my hope that the couples getting married now will build faithful homes among the Jewish people, and that they will smile when telling their grandchildren about their weddings in the time of the coronavirus, and how the experience strengthened them. Mazal tov.

A place to fall

Batsheva Sadan lost both of her parents, Rabbi Eli and Dina Horowitz, when they were murdered in a terrorist attack in their home in Kiryat Arba in 5763 (2003). When she suggests what we should do during the current crisis, she speaks from experience:

"Imagine for a moment that the floor beneath us suddenly collapsed. In fact, this is how we feel now – as if everything has fallen apart. Of course it is terrifying. Now imagine that we knew there was a safety net underneath the floor, so no matter how far we fell, a net would be there to catch us.

"This is the feeling of strength: a deep inner feeling that there is something to hold on to even if everything else collapses. A feeling that there will always be someone to rely on and to whom we can return, someone who knows that we matter. This is confidence in our innate goodness, regardless of our circumstances.

"How do we build such resilience? The days between Rosh HaShana and Yom Kippur teach us that it is always possible to return, and there is always One to Whom we can turn. There is One Who loves us and gives us life anew each day, and is ready to catch us and save us each time we fall.

"And how do we build resilience at home? In exactly the same way: Our children need to know that we will always be by their side. We don't need to either frighten them or make everything seem rosy. We need to be real, and mostly to just be there with them – in their worries, their emotions, and their imaginings as a continuous, stable presence. We need to be their safety net."

Are we dust or stars?

Israel is signing historic peace agreements with the United Arab Emirates, Morocco, Sudan, and Bahrain, and leads the world in its impressive vaccination campaign, yet at the same time it is entering a lockdown because of our frighteningly high COVID-19 morbidity rate. How is it possible to explain simultaneous successes and failures of such magnitude?

Our Sages write about this seeming contradiction as follows: "This nation is compared to dust and to stars. When they descend, they descend to dust, and when they ascend, they ascend to the stars" (Megilla 16a).

Our character is hyperactive and unrestrained, and can be deceptive as we lurch between opposite extremes. Sometimes we are good and generous, optimistic and full of solidarity, and sometimes we are selfish and small-minded, petty, bitter, and uncooperative.

On Rosh HaShana it is customary to say: "Let us be like the head and not the tail." We know how to be a head, we know how to be a tail, and we know how to constantly move between the two. At the beginning of the pandemic, Israel had one of the lowest morbidity rates in the world and now we have one of the highest.

We speak a lot about Israel's division into camps and sectors. It appears now that the pandemic has divided us in a completely different manner, those in the dust and those in the stars. The two types exist within the nation. Indeed, they both exist within each of us, engaged in a struggle. In this time of danger we must decided where we belong. In every one of us, may the impulse of rising to the stars prevail over the impulse to descend to the dust.

Strengthening ourselves with humor

I have heard calls to strengthen ourselves through Torah, and to strengthen ourselves through prayer, but to strengthen ourselves through humor?

Rabbi Gershon Edelstein is one of the foremost Torah sages in Israel, and he is among those who have taken the hardest line in supporting the pandemic restrictions. He was born in the Soviet Union before the Second World War, was orphaned from his mother at a young age, and learned Torah in secret under the oppressive Soviet regime. In nearly one hundred years of life, he has seen the world at its highest and lowest points.

When he was asked for his advice regarding the current crisis, he mentioned one word again and again: humor.

"There must be an atmosphere of good cheer at home. The current situation has certainly brought hardships and we need to carefully observe the restrictions in place, but we can still ensure that an air of pleasantness prevails. Humor – speak with humor; do not be overly serious. Create a cheerful atmosphere, an atmosphere of humor. Not silliness, but humor, so that a pleasant atmosphere will prevail."

How simple this is, but in reality, not so simple. May we be strengthened through humor.

In memory of the pandemic victims

Thousands in Israel have died of COVID-19. All of them deserve to be eulogized with everlasting memories, but here is just one casualty whose spark of life continues to glow among us. Rabbi Benaya Nebenzahl of Jerusalem, fifty-seven years old, passed away after he was infected with COVID-19.

There are many stories about his devotion to his students, his deep concern for everyone, his endless good deeds, and his fascinating educational approach. One story in particular that his family members told about him caught my eye:

Rav Nebenzahl's daughter was preparing to leave for her annual school trip. She asked his advice on whether she should wear the school uniform or regular clothes. Her father asked her, "What do you think most of your friends will wear?" She gave her answer, and then he said, "Wear what you think most of them will not be wearing, so that if one of them wears something different from the rest, she will not feel alone and be embarrassed."

In memory of Rabbi Benaya Nebenzahl
and the thousands of other worlds that have been lost.

Dancing between the table and the bed

In her diaries, Rebbetzin Chana Schneerson, mother of the late Lubavitcher Rebbe, described the Simḥat Torah celebrations that took place during the Soviet era. Her descriptions have served as an inspiration for many during the present pandemic.

The communist regime had opposed the Schneerson family's activities in spreading Judaism, and after interrogations, torture, and a show trial, her husband Rabbi Levi Yitzchak was sent into exile in Kazakhstan, where she joined him. This is what Chana Schneerson wrote about Simḥat Torah in that remote location:

"The day of Simḥat Torah came. A *sefer Torah* was not yet in our possession. My husband and I were all alone in our room. The moment for *Hakafot* arrived when, in the synagogue, the men carry the Torah scrolls and dance with them around the platform where the Torah is read. It is difficult for someone like me to describe the spiritual glow on my husband's face as he began to proclaim in a loud voice: 'You have been shown to know that the Lord, He is God; there is none else beside Him' (Deut. 4:35). He sang the words of the verse to the same tune as he used to do in our city's synagogue in the presence of hundreds of Jews. It seemed that not only did Jews dance each year in our city, but even the stones would dance from the abundance of joy....

"It was with this joy that my husband girded himself here too. He chanted each verse, and after every *Hakafa* he sang and danced – all by himself, of course. Between our table and the bed there was a small area where he danced around and around in circles: 'Pure and upright One, deliver us; benevolent Bestower of goodness, answer us on the day we call.' One could feel the strength of his deep, heartfelt emotion and his desire for pure joy. 'Knower of thoughts, deliver us. Garbed in righteousness, answer us on the day we call.' I sat in a corner on a wooden stool and contemplated the greatness and power of this man's love for Torah as he danced all seven *Hakafot*."

An unusual visit with the police

Moments such as these do not make headlines, but they are events that transpired because of these unusual times in which we find ourselves. Tamar Weizer from Tel Aviv described the following occasion:

"The police visited our synagogue on Shabbat. We were praying in the courtyard outside the synagogue building, as we had been doing in recent weeks, yearning for the taste of Shabbat that we had known before the world went crazy. In truth, I had hesitated about coming to the synagogue this week, but then I remembered that it was the Shabbat when the first Torah portion of the year was to be read, and I wanted to hear the beautiful passages about the creation of the world. So I dressed, organized the children, and made my way to the improvised women's section.

"There were more people than usual in the courtyard. It was the bar mitzva of a secular boy, and all of his excited family stood with us. Suddenly, a policeman and a policewoman arrived. To their credit, they were relatively quiet and I saw how they respectfully lowered the volume on their wallkie-talkies that were attached to their belts. There was a noticeable discomfort among the crowd. Everyone was wearing a mask and keeping a proper distance from one another and yet, despite this, there was unease. The police asked how much longer the prayers would last and it was explained to them that the bar mitzva boy would finish reading the Torah in a few minutes. The policewoman turned to the boy's mother and requested that when the Torah reading was finished, the guests should immediately disperse.

"But then, just before the bar mitzva boy and his family left and the police returned to their patrol car, Rabbi Chaim Eidels, a Gur Hasid, addressed them: 'Friends, please stay with us two more minutes. We would like to thank you from the bottom of our hearts for protecting us, for caring about us. Thank you so much!' He began to clap, and the whole crowd joined him. Then he continued: 'Each Shabbat, we bless the soldiers and the security forces and this Shabbat we would like to bless you in particular.'

"Imagine a policeman and a policewoman standing next to people praying from all sectors of society, with a rabbi wearing a spodik, the tall, black fur hat worn by certain Hasidim on Shabbat, who then recited the prayer: 'May God, who blessed our forefathers Abraham, Isaac, and Jacob, bless our soldiers and security forces, who stand over our land and the cities of our God, from the border of Lebanon to the desert of Egypt, from the Great Sea to the Arava, on land, in the air, and at sea.'"

A Zoom blooper

When it comes to gaffes on Zoom, this one ranks pretty near the top. Sefi Algabish, a school guidance counselor, told me the following story:

"I cannot believe this happened to me. Close your eyes and try to recall that moment when, having spent hours with your young kids driving you crazy, and after managing to restrain yourself over and over again with patience and sensitivity, you finally let it out.

"So today, in the middle of a Zoom course for guidance counselors that dealt with 'The School Climate – Sensitivity and Inclusion,' I decided to call my kids and let them know what I thought about the mess they always make at home. I screamed and scolded and lost my temper, but I forgot to turn off my Zoom microphone, so not only did my children hear the screams, but so did dozens of guidance counselors, my professional colleagues.

"Only when the conference moderator turned to me and requested that I turn off my microphone did I understand the gravity of the incident. In the middle of a course on the very subject of showing sensitivity toward our precious students and children, I did the absolute opposite.

"What can we learn from this? That we are human. It seems to me that this is the most important message during the COVID-19 era, when we fall down and pick ourselves up again a hundred times a day. Bridging the gap between theory and practice is the essence of life. Our entire purpose is to bring idealistic values down to earth and to actually live them. If only. For if I am embarrassed when people outside my home hear me screaming, perhaps I should not scream that way inside it.

"But now that this has happened, I need to direct all the positive words about inclusion, love, and judging favorably toward myself, and not judge myself too harshly.

"Oh, and one more important message: Don't forget to press the mute button when your presentation on Zoom is over!"

Rabbi Lau's bar mitzva

Rabbi Yisrael Meir Lau held a Zoom session with students of the Ort Maalot Yeshiva in the Upper Galilee. He was asked to deliver a message to the boys who had to miss their bar mitzva celebrations due to the pandemic. Rabbi Lau, who was orphaned during the Holocaust, raised in Israel by his uncle, Rabbi Mordechai Fogelman, and eventually became the Ashkenazi Chief Rabbi, told the following story:

"For several months I had been studying the *Shelaḥ* Torah portion in preparation for my bar mitzva. In the synagogue in Kiryat Motzkin there was a Jew who read the Torah every Shabbat, Reb Moishe. The *gabbai* (synagogue warden) forgot to tell him that on this Shabbat, a boy named Yisrael Lau would be celebrating his bar mitzva. And so as I went up and stood on one side of the *bima* (platform where the Torah scroll is read), he went up and stood on the other. The *gabbai* said to him, 'Reb Moishe, today you are not reading; the bar mitzva boy is reading.' And when Reb Moishe said, 'But no one told me,' the *gabbai* answered, 'So now we are telling you.' In response, Reb Moishe said, 'For many years I have volunteered to read the Torah every Shabbat, and now when the synagogue is overflowing with guests from all over the country who came to honor an orphaned bar mitzva boy, a Holocaust survivor, you tell me to leave the *bima*?' He was practically in tears. I was already standing there wearing my tallit, but I saw that he had become emotional, so I went over to his side of the *bima* and said: 'Reb Moishe, I am still young and I hope that I will have many more opportunities in life to read the Torah. I do not want to take away your privilege.' I left the *bima* and Reb Moishe read the Torah portion on my Shabbat bar mitzva."

Since then, Rabbi Lau has indeed received numerous opportunities to read the Torah, to speak, and to appear in public. He finished his message to the students as follows: "I think this was the first mitzva that I observed as a boy taking upon himself the responsibility of being bar mitzva: the mitzva of giving something up. I saw a Jew in anguish, a Jew whose entire honor and pleasure in this world depended on reading the Torah in an overflowing synagogue. Remember, we never lose when we relinquish something. Mazal tov."

What can we still do?

"Shalom Sivan, I am Chaya Golan from Jerusalem. I suddenly noticed the following words that we recite during morning prayers each day: 'These are the things whose fruits we eat in this world but whose full reward awaits us in the World to Come: honoring parents; acts of kindness; arriving early at the house of study, morning and evening; hospitality to strangers; visiting the sick; helping a needy bride; attending to the dead; devotion in prayer; and bringing peace between people – but the study of Torah is equal to them all.'

"These are ten tasks we are meant to do, but in the present situation, five of them are not possible: going out to learn; hosting guests; visiting the sick; helping a needy bride; and escorting the dead. On the other hand, the additional five tasks have become of critical importance: We need to make an extra effort to honor our parents (honoring them when we cannot meet or hug, or when we are isolated with them at home for a prolonged period); acts of kindness (of which there are many, but first of all with family members with whom we are together 24/7); devotion in prayer (examining the meaning of our prayers so that we can pray with more sincerity and intention than usual); bringing peace between people (this is the ideal time for reconciliation and appeasement); and of course, learning Torah in every free moment.

"May we merit to return quickly and joyously to the other five critical tasks as well."

What kind of suffering is this?

"Shalom Sivan, my name is Anat. I was supposed to get married this coming Wednesday. Unfortunately, I found out before Shabbat that I have COVID-19. I completely fell apart. I entered isolation immediately in my room, a room in which my bridal gown and veil and many other accessories had been arranged and were ready for the wedding. I woke up feeling depressed on Friday morning, and then I remembered your interview with the late Chani Weinroth, the young mother who died of cancer, who said: 'We need to separate necessary suffering and unnecessary suffering. Pay attention to what is imposed on us and beyond our control, and what we impose on ourselves and can be changed.' I felt that this had been written for me.

"My necessary suffering was clear: postponing the wedding, entering isolation, putting my relatives in isolation, and treating the headaches and other COVID-19 symptoms that had begun to appear. I would have to cope with all this. But there was also unnecessary suffering that I was likely to impose on myself: crying throughout Shabbat and torturing myself by dreaming about the *Shabbat Kallah* that I had planned with my friends, gazing at all the wedding accessories in my room, not answering friends' phone calls since I did not have the strength, and of course arguing with all the people closest to me and being angry that one of them must have infected me with the virus even though I had been so careful.

"But then I understood that I could prevent all this unnecessary suffering. I got up and began to arrange my room for Shabbat. I spread a white tablecloth on the table and asked for the bouquet that my fiancé had sent. We even began to plan another wedding date. Within a few minutes, I already felt better. The moment I allowed others to help me, I discovered how much they could ease my distress, even from a distance. I am now waiting for the end of the two weeks in isolation with a minimum amount of both necessary and unnecessary suffering, while praying for a happy and healthy wedding."

2020 DOES NOT DESERVE AN X

Time Magazine published its final cover of the year with a red X over the number 2020 and the following message printed beneath: "2020: THE WORST YEAR EVER."

This is, of course, a wild exaggeration. Just for the sake of comparison, during the Second World War, sixty million people were killed, yet *Time Magazine* did not put an X over any of those years. An X was put over Hitler's face because, in the past, the world still knew who the enemy was and fought in solidarity against him. Today, unfortunately, the media prefers to just lower our spirits.

In the book of Genesis, the righteous Joseph suggests another way to contend with crisis. He has plenty of reason to be bitter and disappointed and angry. From a beloved son, he becomes a hated brother who is thrown into a pit, sold to a passing caravan, taken to Egypt, and eventually sent to prison. But Joseph finds meaning and purpose in all the stages of his life, and does not put an X over any of them. He reaches out to help others as well as himself along the way. At the end of his journey, when he reunites with his brothers, he addresses them with the motto that has accompanied him throughout his life: "For it was to preserve life that God sent me before you" (Gen. 45:5). In the face of every hardship and challenge, Joseph always remembered that God had sent him on a special mission – to increase goodness and preserve life.

This perspective will allow us to put an X over *Time Magazine*'s X and see 2020 not as a lost year, but as a time of service and compassionate caring that has helped us preserve life.

The squares of the Western Wall, the squares of Zoom

"Faces on Zoom always look to me like the Western Wall. Lots and lots of squares, like little bricks, a wall of souls. I almost want to put a note between these squares..." said Rabbanit Yemima Mizrachi with a smile, in a meeting she conducted on Zoom with hundreds of girls as part of a "Meeting Up" workshop. Here is some advice she gave them:

"Remember when you were at school in person. There were always girls who were not at the center, but at times like these, it is very easy to forget them altogether. So I ask you to do what Moses did; he left the comfort of the palace and went out to see his brothers who were suffering, to help them. He did not have to do that. It would have been much easier to stay in the palace. But please remember these girls who perhaps no one in the class has spoken to since the beginning of the year.

"Advice for this challenging period: Rabbi Shlomo Wolbe advised us to pray at the beginning of the day about the crises that we already know in advance will come. For example, if I as a mother know that I will be angry with the children who do not attend their classes on Zoom, I pray in advance that instead of getting angry, I should succeed in getting them to cooperate. Then, when the crisis comes, it does not surprise me. I have already prayed about it, so I'm not stressed.

"We have learned this year that evil can be contagious, like this plague is contagious. We must remember that goodness is contagious too. Goodness is also viral, and it must infect the whole world."

Don't wait for the perfect moment

As the lockdowns and the restrictions continue, Jerusalem teacher Yoel Spitz recalls something he learned from Rabbi Adin Steinsaltz, of blessed memory:

"Rabbi Adin once told us: 'There are certain types of people who, if they get a headache or experience any sort of trouble, immediately announce that they are on strike. It's not that they walk around with a sign that says "On strike," but they take a step backward. They wait until their affliction has passed. Meanwhile, they do not pray, study, or attempt to do anything of a serious nature. Now, what comes of this? It's as if such a person says: I am prepared to adopt the form of a Jew. I am prepared to study Torah and to pray. I am ready to run around and do things, but only in a sterile environment without problems or troubles or headaches.

"'To such people, it is important to say that life here on this planet is not built according to this formula. Life is full of issues, troubles, and headaches. If we wait for a beneficial time when conditions are optimal, we will wait our entire lives and do nothing. This means that we need to get going right now – just like this, exactly as we are. We need to get down to work and move, not wait for a more favorable time that will probably never come. If the Holy One, blessed be He wanted just Torah, prayer, and "sterile" good deeds, He has millions of angels to do that work. He created people like us with headaches because he wanted our prayers, our learning, and our good deeds together with our headaches and all our troubles!'

"During this extended lockdown, I have really wanted to say: 'I will be a human being, I promise, but come on, only when this annoying lockdown is over.' And then I was reminded of Rabbi Adin's words and thought: If you are waiting for the ideal time, you will need to wait until you are 120. I hear him whispering in my ears: 'This lockdown, your lockdown, is what God wants. Get moving.'"

A visit to the COVID-19 ward

"Hi, my name is Meital Galor, and I am a resident of Sderot. Tonight I went to visit my father who is hospitalized in the COVID-19 ward, and I returned with two experiences that are important for me to share:

"At first, when I put on the protective gear, I almost suffocated. I felt imprisoned inside with one hat on top of another, overalls, special shoes, masks, and a face shield. It was hot and difficult to cope, but the goal – to see my father for a few minutes – was so important to me that I managed to prevail. Suddenly I understood how much gratitude we should feel toward the medical teams who work with so much dedication for a lot more than a few moments – and not for their father, but for the parents of all of us. Have I given even a moment's thought as to the incredibly difficult working conditions they have endured for nearly a year?

"While we waited outside, a *ḥaredi* man and woman stood next to me in protective gear. I recoiled from them. 'Of course,' I told myself. 'No wonder they are here – they went to a mass funeral and got infected.' But when I overheard a conversation between them, I realized that they were two volunteers who had dropped everything and come to help, simply out of the goodness of their hearts. They divided the patients between them, and even brought one patient hot croissants that he had specially requested. I started to cry. They did not understand what had happened to me, and I began to explain how mistaken I had been about them, and that I had come to visit my hospitalized father. The woman comforted me and said that she had visited my father during the week and had given him some encouragement and cheer.

"Sweating and barely breathing, I started to feel ashamed of myself. I was ashamed of my apathy toward the medical teams, ashamed that I had stereotyped this couple. Thoughts of repentance passed through me that night while I stood in the protective suit. If only the pandemic would cause a mutation within us, a change for the good.

"These words are dedicated to the recovery of my father, Moshe ben Rachel, among all those ailing in Israel."

Matchmaking at a corona hotel

"Shalom, this is Shani Yakobson, twenty-nine years old, and Amir Tzion, thirty-four. On Erev Rosh HaShana, I, Shani, tested positive for COVID-19 and was placed in isolation at a corona hotel, the Carlton Hotel in Nahariya. At exactly the same time, Amir, who works as a hospital nurse, tested positive for the virus and arrived at the same hotel. Both of us entered the new year with an ominous feeling. We went to the hotel in order not to infect our families during the holiday, and we were both in despair over our illness, our isolation, and our lack of certainty.

"On the first of Tishrei, the Day of Judgment which ushers in the new year, we prayed in an improvised synagogue that the heavenly gates would open and bring us good news. While the shofar was blown, both of us prayed that we would merit to build a family home. We were both single but no longer young and had been on numerous dates; we could not have imagined that salvation would come in the dining room of a corona hotel. In retrospect, everything seems so strange. Are we supposed to thank those who infected us? Should we thank the Home Front Command (branch of IDF that managed the corona hotels) for the *shiddukh* (making the match)? Perhaps we should thank the guests at the hotel who stubbornly insisted that we meet, and then left us alone in the dining room so we could talk and get to know each other?

"We have often heard the words of our Sages that 'finding a spouse is as difficult as splitting the Red Sea.' This Shabbat we read in the Torah about the splitting of the Red Sea. We felt this miracle ourselves. We are engaged. We know the situation remains difficult outside, that beyond our bubble, the reality is harsh and painful and frustrating. That's why we wanted to publicize and shout our story to the entire world, to give hope to others during this awful time and to show that even from such darkness, a great light can suddenly grow."

This is the journey

"Mommy, when will corona end?" No mother has the answer to
this question. Merav Sever writes the following about our lack of
certainty:

"If they had told us during the first lockdown last Adar that a
year later we would be in lockdown again, we would have despaired.

"If my customers had known during the first lockdown that
there would be a second and a third, they would have sunk into
a deep depression. They would not have ordered merchandise
and would have closed down their businesses. They would have
stopped fighting and given up.

"If parents had known on the first of September, when the
school year began, that by the time their children received their
report cards at the end of the year they would hardly have been
inside school, they would have been broken and full of anger.

"If I had known at the age of twenty that I would still be single now, I would not have prayed and I would not have had much
hope or desire for living. I would not have been excited about work
and I probably would have fallen by the wayside.

"What allows us breathing space, desire, faith, patience, courage, entrepreneurship – it is precisely the lack of knowledge. That
is what gives us hope. The solution could come at any moment.
There may be an unexpected breakthrough. Perhaps we will soon
be redeemed.

"But true redemption will come when we agree not to try
and control the circumstances of our lives by force, when we recognize that we do not know everything, when we learn to let go.
True redemption of our souls will not come from the desire to
know when the Messiah will come, but rather from living, growing, shouting, hoping, doing good deeds, and waiting. 'And even
though he (the Messiah) may tarry, I will anticipate his arrival
every day' (Hab. 2:3)."

The fonts used in this book are from the Arno family

Maggid Books
The best of contemporary Jewish thought from
Koren Publishers Jerusalem Ltd.